HYRTECENE BARNES

MY JOURNEY
FROM
MISSISSIPPI
TO
NEW YORK

YOU CAN
OVERCOME
ANY
CHALLENGES

This book is dedicated
to my amazing parents,
Mattie and Jim.
To everyone who has been
a part of my journey through life:
This is a heartfelt message
of gratitude and acknowledgement.
Each of you has played
a vital role in shaping my
experiences, guiding my path,
and helping me
become the person
I am today.
Your support, kindness,
and influence have
made a lasting impact,
and I am deeply
thankful for every
moment we've shared.

In this picture is my sister, my mom and me on the right side

The gift, the journey, a cherished Life.

In morning's light, our stories begin,
With dreams like whispers, precious within.
Each step we take, both big and small,
Shapes our path and matters to all.
With laughter and joy, we learn how to thrive,
In moments of struggle, we feel alive.
Through shadows and peaks, we follow our dreams,
Finding strength in the journey, or so it seems.
Friends by our side, with hearts open wide,
Together we navigate life's changing tide.
As time flows on, love makes us strong,
The journey of life is where we belong.
So cherish each moment, both bitter and sweet,
For every step is what makes life complete.
With love as our compass, hope as our guide,
The gift that we create is the journey inside.

My Family

In the heart of Jackson, Mississippi, where the cold winds of 1934 carried the whispers of struggle and survival, my journey began. This memoir is a collection of stories stitched together from the fabric of my childhood, filled with the joys and sorrows that shaped me.

The story here isn't just for myself but for those who may find solace in these pages - those who have faced adversity, navigated the complexities of love, and loss, and emerged stronger on the other side.

As a little girl, my life was marked by the warmth of my father's love and the painful absence that followed. I grew up in a world steeped in segregation and the shadows of the Great Depression. I learned early on the importance of family, the strength found in love, and the resilience that can blossom even in the face of unimaginable hardship.

Through this memoir, I invite you into my story - a tale of a girl who danced between the light and darkness, finding hope in the most unlikely places. These pages hold my truth, my heart, and the lessons that life has taught me along the way. It is a journey of reflection, healing, and the unbreakable bonds of family.

A picture a smile tells a story

The Beginning

This is the beginning of my memoir, a journey through my family's history that has been shaped by both struggle and resilience. Our story is woven with threads of hardship, particularly the painful legacy of slavery, which has left deep scars on African American families like mine. While slavery ended many years ago, its absence still echoes in our lives today, reminding us of the pain and separation it caused.

Growing up, my mother shared countless stories about our ancestry, especially her experiences in Mississippi. Her words painted vivid pictures of a time marked by the harsh realities of the Jim Crow Laws. These unjust laws enforced racial segregation and discrimination, dividing communities and treating Black people as inferior.

In the southern states where we lived, these laws dictated that Black and white individuals had to use separate schools, transportation, restrooms, and restaurants. Unfortunately, the facilities provided for Black people were often of much lower quality, stripping away basic dignity and respect.

The effects of these laws reached far beyond just daily inconviences; they limited our voting rights, restricted access to education and good jobs, and created a system of inequality that felt inescapable. The name "Jim Crow" itself comes from a minstrel character that mocked Black people, highlighting the cruelty of a society built on prejudice.

Yet, even in the face of such overwhelming odds, there were those who refused to stay silent. Brave individuals rose up to challenge these discriminatory laws, leading to the monumental changes brought about by the Civil Rights Act of 1964 and the Voting Rights Act of 1965. Their courage shines brightly against the backdrop of our history, reminding us of the power of resilience and hope.

This is not just my story; it is the story of my family - a testament to the strength we carry forward. As I reflect on this journey, I do so with a full heart, grateful for the lessons learned and the fierce spirit that binds us through generations. Together, we navigate the complexities of life, honoring the past while striving for a brighter future.

Born in Jackson Mississippi

I was born in December 1934, when Franklin D. Roosevelt was President of the United States. A difficult time in history when the world was facing the cold reality of the Great Depression. Alongside these economic challenges, I also faced the harsh realities of systemic racism and discrimination.

The world outside was harsh, and home felt heavy with unspoken words. I remember so vividly the day my dad passed away when I was six years old. It was as if the sun had dimmed for me, casting a shadow over my young heart. My dad was my protector, my hero, and losing him felt like losing a piece of myself. He had a way of making me feel cherished and special. He had a love that wrapped around me like a warm blanket, reminding me that I mattered in a world that sometimes seemed unforgiving.

After he was gone, my mom's words cut deep into my spirit. I overheard her telling a neighbor that I was a mistake, and in that moment, I felt the weight of her disappointment pressing down on me. Growing up, that sting lingered, a shadow that seemed to follow me wherever I went. My sister echoed those feelings, and I often felt as if I was living in a place where love was scarce. They made me feel unwanted, as if I didn't truly belong in my own family. But I was not alone in my heartache. My brother always stood by my side, his presence a comforting shield against the harshness of the world. He was my protector, the one who reminded me of my worth when I was surrounded by doubt.

Whenever I felt small and invisible, he was there to lift me up, encouraging me to be brave. It was in those moments that I learned the power of family and the strength of unconditional love. Despite the pain of losing my dad and the struggles I faced at home, I found pockets of joy in my childhood. I remember playing outside with my brother, our laughter cutting through the gloom. He made the world feel brighter, even during the darkest days. I treasured the stories my dad used to tell, and I would often close my eyes, imagining his warm smile and the sound of his voice. Those memories kept my heart aglow even when I felt lost.

As the years went by, I realized that the scars from my childhood would always be a part of me, but they didn't have to define me. I learned to embrace my resilience, to let my dad's love be the foundation upon which I built my life. I understood that even amidst adversity, I had the power to create my own happiness. Each day, I chose to rise above the hurtful words and feelings of being unwanted. I sought out the beauty in everyday moments, discovering joy in the simplest things–a warm hug from my brother, a sunny day, or a kind word from a neighbor. My brother's unwavering support showed me that love can exist even when it feels scarce.

Through it all, I grew stronger. I realized that although I had faced challenges that could have broken me, I had the power to rise, to stand tall, and to love fiercely. The name Hyrtecene began to mean something different to me–it became a symbol of my journey, a reminder that I was worthy of love and happiness, despite the voices that tried to tell me otherwise. As I continue to reflect on my life, I carry my dad's love with me as a guiding light. My story, filled with struggles and triumphs, reminds me that I can overcome anything life throws my way. I hope to inspire others to find their strength and redefine their own stories, reminding them that they are worthy of love, just as I am.

The loss of my dad in December 1940 left an indelible mark on my family, uprooting the foundation of love and security he had built. His absence felt like a gaping hole in our lives, a void that left us struggling to navigate the world without his guiding hand. In the heart of a difficult time, where survival was a daily challenge, we had to face not only the grieving process but also the harsh realities of life during segregation.

With my dad gone, the burden of provision fell on my mom's shoulders. She was left to raise three children in a society where opportunities were limited and the odds were stacked against us. The Great Depression still loomed over our lives, making even the most basic necessities a struggle to obtain. It was a time when many families faced hunger, and we were no different. I remember the empty cupboards and the worry etched into my mom's face as she tried to stretch whatever little food we had.

In a world divided by race, our family bore the brunt of the discrimination that surrounded us. My mixed heritage, being a black child with a father of Irish descent, added another layer of complexity to our lives. In a segregated society, the color of our skin dictated where we could go, who we could interact with, and what we could aspire to become. This made our grief even more profound, as society showed its indifference to our suffering, often making us feel invisible.

The struggle to survive each day was exhausting. I watched my mom work tirelessly, juggling multiple jobs just to put food on the table. But even with her hard work, there were days when we went to bed hungry. My sister, burdened with her own sadness, struggled to find comfort, often echoing our mom's feelings of despair. I felt the weight of their disappointment, the perception that I was a burden on top of everything else they were facing.

Yet even in the darkest times, the bond between my brother and I became a source of strength. He stepped up to protect me, reassuring me that I wasn't alone. In our small moments of play, we created our secret world – a place free of the harsh realities we faced every day. But outside our bubble, life was hard, and every day was a battle. Segregation meant we walked down separate sidewalks, that we were treated differently in shops and schools. I remember feeling so angry and confused–why were we seen as less worthy simply because of our skin color? It felt unjust, especially when I just wanted to be treated like everyone else.

Our challenges were compounded by the fear and uncertainty in the air. As a young girl, I couldn't fully understand why the world seemed so hard on us, or why kindness felt like a rarity. I stood at the crossroads of grief and growing up, and each day was a reminder of the realities we had to face. Despite it all, my dad's memory lived on in the stories we told. We spoke of his love, his laughter, and the way he made everything feel right. My brother and I started to mimic his gestures, his laughter and in those moments, it felt like he was with us again. Such memories wrapped around me like a hug, deepening my resolve to survive, to honor his legacy.

Through the eyes of a child, I learned valuable lessons from these hardships. I discovered the importance of compassion and the strength of family bonds. I realized that, even when times were tough and life felt unfair, the love we shared could carry us through. We were each other's light in a world plagued by shadows. Though my dad was gone, his spirit echoed in our hearts, guiding me as I navigated through a difficult childhood. Life was hard, but I learned early on that resilience lived within me, just waiting for the right moment to shine. And with every challenge faced, I came closer to understanding my place in this complex world, determined to rise above the sorrows and create a future filled with love and hope.

The tragedy of my dad's death was not just in losing him; it was in the way he left us. He died in a hospital far away from home, and we were many miles apart when it happened. My mom received the devastating news through a small, cold telegram that would change our lives forever. The words were so brief, almost harsh in their simplicity: "My husband, Jim Roper has died and he is buried." How could this be? I remember my mom's face–the shock, the disbelief as she absorbed those painful words. There was no comfort, no farewell, and certainly no chance for us to say goodbye. I felt a swirl of confusion and sorrow. Who had buried my dad? Why was he so far away? We didn't even know where he lay to rest. In that moment, I realized we were left with nothing but questions and an ache that echoed in our hearts.

This profound loss was devastating for all of us. It shattered our family and plunged us deeper into the already murky waters of grief and despair. My mom, overwhelmed by her own sadness and the weight of responsibility, struggled to provide for us as she grappled with the loss of the love of her life.

In a world overcome by prejudice, segregation, and the lingering effects of the Great Depression, we felt more than just sorrow; we felt the sting of being treated less than human. Our struggles were compounded by the societal barriers that surrounded us. Segregation imposed a harsh reality—our existence was dictated by the color of our skin. We were often looked down upon, facing biases at every turn. The grief of losing my dad was intertwined with the pain of societal rejection, making it hard to breathe sometimes, as if the world itself was closing in on us.

As my mom battled her own demons, my sister struggled in her own way. She, too, felt the weight of our dad's absence and the harshness of life. I often found myself trying to soothe her, feeling the role of protector shift once again. My brother and I learned from each other, grappling with our sadness in the shadows of a society that seemed indifferent to our plight.

The absence of our dad left an emptiness that echoed throughout our home. We missed his laughter, his warmth, and the way he made us feel safe. As the days turned into weeks and the weeks into months, I felt that emptiness grow. I wondered if my dad would have wanted us to be so sad—to feel less than, to struggle against a world that often felt cruel and unforgiving.

In our hearts, we knew he was gone, but we also carried the hope that came with love. Even though society tried to rob us of our dignity, my brother and I found solace in our memories of him. We recalled his stories, the way he would play with us, and how he filled our home with joy. Those moments became our treasures; a flicker of light in our darkest hours. Yet, the unknowing hung heavily over us like a dark cloud. Not knowing where my dad had been buried felt like an open wound, a missing piece of closure we so desperately needed. It was hard to comprehend the idea that a man who had given us so much joy was now just a name lost to the winds of distance and prejudice.

How could this happen? Why did the world feel so unfair when all we wanted was to honor his memory properly and keep him close to our hearts? I couldn't help but feel anger bubbling up within me—a righteous anger against a world that seemed to care so little, treating us like shadows in a society that valued others more than it valued us. But as painful and heavy as this tragedy was, it also forged something inside me, a resolve to rise above the challenges. I knew that my dad would have wanted us to fight for our place in the world, to live boldly and honor his memory with love and courage. Through the sorrow, I would strive to create a legacy that honored my dad's love, a legacy unclouded by the prejudice we faced.

In the midst of despair, I learned that we could carve our truth from the mess of grief and hardship. Though my dad was gone, his spirit remained woven into the fabric of who I was becoming, teaching me to embrace life even when it was hard. I became determined to fight for a future that embraced love, equality, and compassion–not just for myself, but for everyone who felt the sting of injustice.

As the years went by, I began to piece together fragments of my dad's life that had remained hidden from me during my childhood. Through whispers shared among my mom, family, and neighbors, I learned that my dad had epilepsy. This revelation struck me hard. I remember him as a strong man, always out working hard in public service, never showing any sign of weakness or illness. How could I not have known?

As a little girl, I was blissfully unaware of the struggles he faced. I would see him come home tired but happy, ready to play with us or tell us stories to brighten our days. I never saw the pain he must have endured or the challenges posed by his condition. It seemed impossible that my dad had fought such a private battle while carrying the weight of the world on his shoulders.

When I learned about his epilepsy, a sense of guilt washed over me. What could I have done to help my daddy if I had only known? I thought back to my childhood—wondering if there were moments when he struggled silently, masked by his unwavering love for us. I felt helpless, wishing I could have been there for him in ways I couldn't understand back then. But the weight of that realization pressed heavily on my small shoulders.

How many times had he hidden his struggles to stay strong for our family? I wished I had been able to support him, to help him through the moments when he must have felt so alone. My heart ached with the thought of him fighting in silence, battling an illness that was invisible to my young eyes. It was hard to understand how he could be both my hero and someone facing such a challenging condition.

Yet, in my confusion, I also found a deeper understanding of my dad's strength. His ability to mask his struggles and continue working hard for our family was a testament to his character. He was not only my dad but also a warrior fighting his own battles while trying to provide for us. This realization changed how I saw him; he was even more remarkable in my eyes. Now, knowing what I know, I wanted to cherish his memory not only as my loving father but also as a man who overcame adversity every single day. I wanted to honor him by being strong and resilient in my own life, just like he had been. I could feel his spirit encouraging me, reminding me that even in the face of hardships, love and determination could prevail. As I reflected on my childhood, I learned to embrace my feelings—both of sadness and gratitude. Yes, it hurt to think I had been unaware of my father's struggles, but it also filled me with love and respect for the man he was. I focused on the great moments we shared, the lessons he taught me, and how his love shaped who I had become.

Through my father's story, I realized that everyone bears invisible battles. I learned to carry this understanding in my heart as I forged my path forward, vowing never to take the love of family for granted again. From that point on, I hoped to honor my father's legacy by standing up for others who might be fighting their own invisible battles, reminding them that they are not alone. As I grew older, the weight of reality settled upon my small shoulders, casting a long shadow over my childhood. By 1944, the struggles of life in Jackson, Mississippi, felt increasingly palpable. I watched my mom navigate the harsh landscape of our existence with relentless determination; each day was a testament to her strength and resilience. The labor she undertook was grueling, the work demanding and often undervalued.

From dawn until dusk, my mom worked multiple jobs—cleaning houses, doing laundry for wealthier families, and taking on any other tasks that could bring in a few coins to provide for me and my siblings. The early morning light would often find her slipping out the front door, her silhouette framed against the pale glow of the rising sun. I remember those mornings vividly, the quiet of the house broken only by the soft sounds of her movements and the distant calls of birds heralding the new day. Each job left her more exhausted than the last, but she never complained. Her relentless commitment to our family was a lesson in sacrifice that I absorbed silently. Every evening, weary but determined, she would return home to prepare meals. The kitchen would fill with the aroma of whatever feast she had crafted from the simplest and most affordable ingredients. On the table, a pot of rice or a small portion of beans often accompanied whatever meat she could afford, sometimes just a single piece shared among us. I watched in fascination as she transformed these basic elements into something nourishing, pouring all her energy into making meals that would feed not only our bodies but our spirits, too.

As she stirred the pot or cut the vegetables, I marveled at how she infused a sense of warmth and love into our simple dinners, as if each ingredient carried a piece of her heart. The way she plated the food, even on the roughest of days, held a kind of artistry within the confines of our everyday life. She would arrange everything with care, placing a sprig of fresh herbs on top, a small gesture that felt abundant amid our scarcity. It was in those simple moments that I felt a profound admiration for her, a powerful sense of gratitude mingled with an ache in my heart for the heavy burdens she bore. I sensed the weight of her worries in the lines of her face, each wrinkle a testament to the years of hard work and sleepless nights. While I delighted in the meals she prepared, I also couldn't help but notice the tiredness in her eyes, that flicker of exhaustion that seemed to intensify as the days turned into weeks and months. It was a realization that came slowly but inevitably; my mother was not just an unwavering pillar of strength, but also a woman fighting against the erosive tides of circumstance, her spirit undaunted despite the challenges that lay before us.

As I sat at the table, my siblings and I would gather around, laughter and chatter spilling over even the toughest of days. There was comfort in our shared moments, a reminder that we were together in this struggle. My mother would often join in our conversations, her smile revealing a fleeting glimpse of joy beneath her weariness. I cherished these nights, where we could share not only the food she had painstakingly prepared but also stories of our day, dreams for tomorrow, and laughter that echoed against the walls of our home. Yet, even as we ate together, I could see the shadows of her worries lingering just beyond the light of our little kitchen. The thought that persisted in my mind was the hope—the hope that one day things would be different. Each meal became a ritual of resilience, a sanctuary where our dreams could coexist with our harsh realities. In those moments together, I felt the weight of my mother's burdens but also the strength of her love, a powerful force that provided a flicker of hope amidst the shadows cast by our circumstances.

My mom had always been our pillar of strength, the unwavering force that held our little family together through thick and thin. But as the months turned into years, I began to see the toll that chronic overwork and the relentless stress of providing for three children took on her health. Those long hours spent cleaning homes and working menial jobs drained her energy, leaving her looking increasingly exhausted and frail. The radiant spark that once characterized her spirit dimmed, shadowed by the harsh realities of life that constantly pressed down upon her. I could sense the shift, the palpable change that crept into our home like a thief in the night. The deep circles under her eyes were a constant reminder of her sleepless nights, the result of both labor and worry. Mornings when she awoke, I would watch her as she stood in front of the mirror, brushing her hair and tying it back. The reflection staring back at me was not the vibrant woman I remembered. Instead, it was a woman weighed down by the burdens she bore, moving slower and more carefully with each passing day, as though simply standing upright required all of her remaining strength.

There were moments when she would sit at the kitchen table, a slight tremor in her hands as she folded the laundry or prepared meals. I felt an overwhelming urge to reach out, to take the tasks from her, to ease her burden if only for a moment. But in her eyes, I could detect the fierce stubbornness that defined her—she refused to show weakness, determined to keep the household running, even as it began to feel like a fragile house of cards.

I tried to help whenever I could, taking on more chores around the house. I would wash the dishes or sweep the floors, hoping that it would lighten her load. During those afternoons, I often found myself daydreaming about a world where my mom could rest, where she could sit in the sun with a book, free from the duties that anchored her to our reality. But the dreams would flutter away like leaves in the wind, replaced by the immediate need to make our lives a little easier and a little brighter. Yet, in witnessing her struggles, my admiration only deepened. She was the embodiment of resilience, pushing through each day for us, regardless of the cost to her own well-being. She would often make light of her fatigue, cracking jokes to draw smiles from my siblings and me. "You think I'm tired? Just wait until you have kids of your own!" she'd laugh, her voice buoyant despite the exhaustion painted on her face. Those moments gave me a glimpse into her indomitable spirit, a spirit that continued to fight, even when it felt like the fight was wearing her down.

But there were also days when the weight of her reality was too much for her to mask. On those days, she would sit quietly, perhaps staring out the window, lost in thoughts we were too young to comprehend. I would watch her then, a deep ache settling in my heart as I realized that the emotional toll was just as significant as the physical. Her eyes would glaze over, filled with a distant sadness that made it clear she was carrying more than just the weight of our needs; she was also bearing the weight of her unfulfilled dreams. Each time I saw those signs of weariness, a knot formed in my stomach, and I wished with all my being that I could take her burdens and carry them myself. I wanted to tell her that she didn't have to do it all alone, that we were a team, but the words often felt stuck in my throat. Instead, I would quietly resolve to work harder, to study more diligently, to find a way to lift her up as she had always done for us.

Little did I know, those years of watching and learning would shape me into someone determined to break the cycle of hardship—a desire that would fuel my resolve in the years to come. As her health waned, I felt an urgency rising within me, an understanding that I would carry her strength with me always, and one day, I would use it to create a brighter future. As my mother's health continued to decline, the weight of our family's grief became an anchor that pulled us deeper into sorrow. The day she was hospitalized felt like the ground had fallen away beneath us. I could hardly process the emotions swirling within me: fear, confusion, and the heavy sense of loss that hovered just beyond our doorstep. My siblings and I stood together, staring at the hospital entrance, wishing we could bring her back to us, back to the life we had clung to so fiercely. In her absence, we found ourselves in the reluctant care of our uncle. He had always loomed large in our lives, a figure of authority and strength, but his tenderness had been overshadowed by the harsh realities we faced. I barely knew him as a person; he was more a concept of family, and now he had become our guardian during this chaotic time. The very idea of living under his roof filled me with a mix of hope and trepidation, and I could see that my siblings shared my unease.

Uncle had good intentions, of that I was sure. He tried to provide for us, his slightly awkward attempts at care revealing his own discomfort with the situation. He managed to prepare simple meals, often lacking the warmth of my mother's cooking, yet there was an earnestness in his efforts that I admired. The evenings spent at the dining table felt different—hushed and careful, as if we were afraid the slightest misstep would fracture the fragile peace hanging over us. Each bite was a reminder of who was missing, and the silence filled with what-ifs that lingered in the air. Though he did his best, the adjustment was fraught with difficulties, each day layered with uncertainties that loomed over our already fragile existence. Our uncle was stern and serious, a man shaped by hard times, and I could see the way the stress etched deeper lines into his forehead. He tried to talk to us about our mother, sharing stories I had never heard, attempting to bridge the gaps left by her absence, but the joy in those memories felt muted. They were a bittersweet reminder of what we had lost, a past I desperately wanted to reclaim.

During those long nights, as the world outside faded into darkness, I would often lie awake in the small room I shared with my siblings, my thoughts racing like a storm inside my head. Uncertainty wrapped itself around me, tighter than any blanket, squeezing out the comfort I once felt in our home. I wondered how long it would be before our mother came back to us and whether she would be the same when she did. Every slight creak of the house felt magnified, as if the very walls held their breath in waiting, just like us. As time passed, I noticed my siblings retreating into their own worlds, I found myself stepping up more and more each day, a role I hadn't anticipated taking on at such a young age. I cooked simple meals when my Uncle was busy at work. Each responsibility felt heavy, a reminder of how drastically our lives had changed. But through my efforts, I also hoped to honor her, to keep the essence of our family alive even as we stood at the precipice of an uncertain future.

Each day was a test of our resilience, and though doubts flickered at the edges, I held onto the belief that we would emerge from this time stronger. Through whispered prayers into the dark and dreams that wove together my mother's spirit with our shared love, I resolved to gather us together, to hold us tight against the crushing weight of sorrow, and to remember that even in the midst of loss, there was still love to carry us forward. I felt a twinge of anxiety in my stomach as we settled into our uncle's home, a place that felt distant and unfamiliar amid the chaos of our lives. His attempts at providing care were earnest, but they lacked the warmth of a mother's love, and I couldn't help but feel a profound sense of displacement. The routine I had crafted with my mother had been uprooted, leaving me longing for the semblance of normalcy that had been abruptly torn away from us.

As we adjusted to this new reality, the weight of unanswered questions hovered in the air like a thick fog. We had never been given the chance to grieve our father properly; the finality of his death had been sealed in the simple, chilling telegram that stated nothing more than he had died in the hospital. It provided no details, no solace—an absence of context that left us reeling and struggling to understand how to make sense of it all.

I often found myself replaying memories of my father, clinging to the laughter and warmth he had brought into our lives. Yet, the painful reality of never having said goodbye loomed large over those recollections. The telegram's lack of detail gnawed at my mind, a constant reminder that we had been robbed of closure. We had not even been allowed to participate in his burial; it felt as though he had been taken from us twice—first by death and then by the very system that governed our lives, leaving us with a hollow ache in our hearts.

In whispered tones, my siblings and I would share our unspoken fears late at night, lying awake under the same blankets, our faces illuminated by the gentle glow of the moonlight streaming through the window. The truth lingered heavily between us—the understanding that our father had been a man in a society that often inflicted violence and indifference upon our community. With that understanding came the harsh knowledge that we were painfully powerless in a world that refused to see us fully or treat us with dignity.

My uncle, though well-meaning, often echoed the sentiments fed to us from the world outside—a rigid understanding of our place in society. He dictated routines and expectations that felt stifling, stripping away the freedom I had experienced in my mother's care. "You need to do what you're told," he would say, his voice gruff. "There are rules. Follow them." These words weighed heavily on me, a stark contrast to the love that had once been given freely. The essence of choice—a luxury denied to us—made every decision feel dictated rather than consensual, further cultivating the sense of loss that permeated our lives.

Days turned into weeks, and despite my uncle's attempts at structure, the absence of my mother created a void that could not be filled. My siblings and I felt the strain of grief pressing down upon us, suffocating our spirit. While at school, I became acutely aware of the differences that distanced us from our peers. Our clothing was threadbare, and our circumstances were a constant reminder of our economic struggle. The laughter and joy that echoed around us served only to highlight our isolation.

Picking Cotton Is Hard Work

As the days turned into weeks, my life took yet another turn when my uncle decided it was time for me to contribute more directly to the household. With my mother still in the hospital and the financial strain becoming more pronounced, he took me out to pick cotton. The thought filled me with dread, but I also felt an undeniable sense of responsibility to help my family however I could.

Under the blistering sun, the fields stretched endlessly before me, an ocean of green and brown punctuated by the soft white tufts of cotton ready to be harvested. My heart raced as we stepped onto the land, each step echoing with the weight of the reality that had settled upon us. The scent of the soil mixed with the sweat on my brow as the harsh truth of manual labor greeted me with unyielding intensity.

My uncle explained what to do, his voice a mixture of frustration and necessity. "You've got to keep up, sweet child, that was my nickname. This is how we make ends meet," he said sharply, casting a wary glance at me. I nodded, determination replacing my initial dread as I tried to shake off the nervousness that wrapped itself around me.

As we began working, I quickly discovered the gruesomeness of the task. Bending low to the ground, I plucked the cotton from the plants, my fingers scratched by the rough leaves and thorny stalks. The sun beat down on me relentlessly, sweat pouring down my back and mixing with the dirt that caked on my skin. The labor was hard; each movement was deliberate yet exhausting, forcing me to dig deep into my reserves of strength just to keep pace with my uncle.

For hours, I toiled beside him, the sun mercilessly roasting my skin, my hands growing sore and raw from the constant pulling of the cotton bolls. I watched as other workers joined us in the fields, their faces weary yet familiar, seasoned by the labor that had etched lines of hardship into their skin. This was a grim reality that echoed through generations, a cycle of toil that had defined our community for far too long.

I could hear muffled conversations around me, the sounds of laughter and camaraderie offering fleeting moments of relief from the grueling work. Yet, there was also an undercurrent of sorrow—the burdens shared in the whispers of old stories, tales of struggles and triumphs that spoke to the resilience of our people. In those moments of connection, I found a sense of solidarity, the acknowledgment that we were all part of something greater, tied together by shared experience and history. But as the hours dragged on and fatigue began to grip my body, I felt the tears prick my eyes, blinding me from the task at hand. The realization weighed heavily on me: this was our life now, filled with labor and hardship, with the ache of loss and sorrow stitched into every fiber of our being. I longed for the innocent days of laughter with my father, a time when the hardest work I faced was cleaning my room or helping my mother in the kitchen.

Amidst the exhaustion, my uncle's sharp voice cut through my thoughts. "Keep moving! We don't have all day!" He was pushing me to work faster, but all I could feel was the overwhelming weight of it all—the struggles piled high, threatening to crush my spirit.

As the sun began to sink below the horizon, casting long shadows across the fields, I allowed myself a moment to breathe. I paused for just a breath—a brief escape from the relentless toil—before rejoining my uncle in the struggle to fill the sacks. My heart ached from the weight of the cotton I carried, as if it mirrored the heaviness in my chest.

Finally, after what felt like a lifetime, day turned to dusk and the filled sacks were gathered together. My body was exhausted, my muscles aching and my spirit bruised, but within me was a flicker of pride—I had faced this challenge head-on, despite its brutality. I was a part of the labor, contributing to my family's survival, even as a part of me longed for reprieve. On the walk home, I trudged alongside my uncle, the silent weight of the day hanging heavily between us. It was a moment filled with an understanding deeper than words could convey. Despite the hardships, despite the weariness both physical and emotional, we were walking home together—survivors navigating a world that sought to devalue us.

In those tears and aching muscles, I began to see the raw tenacity that resided within me; the understanding that even amidst the struggle, life pressed forward. With each passing day, I would find ways to honor my father's memory and carry my family's legacy through the hardships we faced. And as I closed my eyes later that night, worn but resolute, I vowed to continue working toward a future filled with hope, drawing strength from the connections we shared and the love that intertwined our lives within the fabric of our community.

When my mother was finally released from the hospital, a wave of joy washed over our home. The day felt electric, a marked change from the somber shadows that had loomed since her absence. I could hardly hold back my excitement as I waited by the door, my heart pounding in my chest. When the door creaked open, and my mother stepped inside, I rushed into her arms, enveloping her in a fierce embrace that spoke volumes of our love and longing.

"Mom! You're home!" I exclaimed, tears of happiness streaming down my cheeks. My mother, though visibly weary and a bit frail, radiated warmth as she held us close, breathing in the familiar scent of our home, which felt all too precious after her time away.

In the days that followed, I grasped every opportunity to help my mother recover, eager to ease her burden and restore some sense of normalcy to our lives. I devoted myself to domestic duties with unwavering enthusiasm—sweeping the floors, washing dishes, and organizing the meager supplies we had. Each task embraced my mother's presence, a tribute to the strength that had seemed so fragile during her illness.

I felt a certain happiness in nurturing the home, finding comfort in the rhythm of our daily lives. "Let me make dinner tonight, Mom!" I said one evening, determined to surprise her with a special meal. My mother smiled softly, pride in her eyes as she watched me bounce around the kitchen. We chatted about everything and nothing, filling the space with laughter, and for a moment, it felt as if the shadows were lifting.

Meanwhile, my brother and sister took on other chores to keep our family afloat, determined to do their part in preserving the fragile harmony we had fought to rebuild. My brother helped with outdoor tasks, tending to what little we could grow in our small yard, learning how to nurture plants that would provide us with food. He carried a weight of responsibility, and though he sometimes struggled under the burden, he did so with an unwavering determination to support the family.

My sister, on the other hand, assumed other chores around the home. Together, we embraced the idea that survival depended on collaboration, each of us offering a piece of the puzzle to create a semblance of stability amid the chaos of our lives. As days turned into weeks, our home began to hum with a newfound vibrancy. I observed how mom gradually regained strength, her spirit returning like spring after a long winter. We shared smiles over the dinner table, where laughter began to fill the air, breathing life into our once-silent home. In those small moments together, we forged the resilient thread of connection that bound us, overflowing with determination to overcome whatever struggles lay ahead.

Yet, there were still echoes of loss that lingered in the background. We would sometimes gather in the evenings, the silence stretching between us as we remembered my father—the man who had brought so much joy into our lives. I would sometimes find myself lost in thought, feeling a mixture of joy and heartache as I reminisced about the stories he had told, the warmth of his embrace, and the laughter we had shared. In those moments, mom would share soft stories, glancing at me with a look of understanding.

"Your father would have loved this, would have been so proud of all of you," she would say softly, her voice tinged with both love and sadness. I would nod, tears welling up in my eyes—but I also felt a sense of grace in the way we honored his legacy with every meal cooked, every evening spent together.

Despite the hardships that remained—economic struggle, the scars of grief, and the societal challenges we faced—we found small victories woven into the fabric of our lives. We learned to take joy in the simple moments, recognizing that our love was a force equally capable of lifting us through sorrow.

With each passing day, as laughter filled our home and shadows receded, I felt a sense of resolve growing within me. As a family, we were learning to not only endure but to thrive in the face of adversity. And with my mother home, I found renewed hope for a future where love could conquer life's trials, a future that honored our past while embracing the possibilities ahead. In the warmth of our renewed togetherness, I vowed to continue writing our story—a narrative of resilience, unity, and an unwavering spirit that could weather any storm.

I often felt the weight of hardship pressing down on our household. The financial strains were a constant presence, a stark reminder of the battles we faced every day. With limited income and mounting bills, I found myself balancing my childhood responsibilities with the harsh realities of domestic work. The burden seems heavier than before, and while I wanted nothing more than to help mom, each chore reminded me of the difficulties we were navigating together.

My sister, dealing with the loss of our dad, often reacted by challenging the household rules. Her grief expressed itself through her rebellious behavior, turning her into a storm as she tried to regain some control in a world that felt completely out of order. "Why should I have to do what you say?" she would argue with our mom, the frustration spilling over in sharp words that cut the air between them. It was a struggle for autonomy amidst a backdrop of sorrow—my sister trying desperately to assert herself in a world where everything seemed uncertain.

I witnessed the rift growing, the tension threading through the very fabric of our lives. My heart ached as I saw my mom's face crumple under the weight of those arguments, a familiar look of despair crossing her features. I wanted to shield her from the pain my sister's voice brought, but I also understood the wildness that hung in the air, the grief that fed our family's tension.

My brother, stepping into the role of the "man of the house," tried to take on the responsibility of mediating the growing conflicts. With each argument that escalated, he grew more frustrated, struggling to find a way to bridge the gap between our rebellious sister and our emotionally vulnerable mom. "You shouldn't talk to Mom that way!" he'd say, his voice firm and unwavering, trying to impose order over the chaos.

But his efforts often met resistance. My sister would roll her eyes, challenging his authority as if that were the only way to reclaim her sense of self. "You're not Dad!

You can't tell me what to do!" she would retort, her voice laced with a mix of anger and sorrow—a reminder that our dad was no longer there to guide us, leaving behind a void that no amount of bravado could fill.

I felt trapped in the middle of these family dynamics—caught between the desire to alleviate mom's burdens and the tumult caused by my siblings. Every time my sister lashed out, it felt like fire igniting our home. The warmth we had fought to build was threatened by the flames of anger and grief, and I sometimes felt powerless against the tides of emotion crashing around me.

In those conflicted moments, I would steal away to my room, seeking solace in my drawings. I filled pages with scenes of happiness and family togetherness, hoping to translate the chaos around me into something peaceful. The illustrations became my therapy, a canvas where love and connection could flourish free from the strife I felt in my home. With each stroke of my pencil, I channeled my frustration, longing for a sense of unity amidst the wreckage of our lives.

Yet as the days wore on, I also knew we had to address the wounds left from our father's death. The road to healing was turbulent, filled with jagged peaks of pain and valleys of confusion. I recognized that each family member was navigating their own understanding of loss, and with that came the need to communicate our struggles—though finding the words felt nearly impossible at times.

During one particularly tense evening, I finally mustered the courage to speak up. It was the first time in a long while that we had sat around the dinner table without an argument breaking the peace. I looked at my brother, then my sister and mom, my heart pounding as I cleared my throat. "Can we just talk? Like, really talk?" I asked, my voice barely above a whisper.

My siblings looked at each other, surprised by the suddenness of my request. Mom, resting her eyes, nodded gently, encouraging me. I felt a surge of determination, a flicker of hope igniting within me as I took a deep breath. "We've all lost so much," I began, my voice shaking slightly. "I know we're hurting, each of us in our own way. But pushing each other away won't help. We need to be together, even if it's hard."

My sister's expression softened as if slowly realizing I was speaking from a place of empathy, while my brother sighed deeply, understanding the weight of our collective pain. Mom wiped the corner of her eye, an acknowledgment of the turmoil that had taken root within our hearts.

In that moment of vulnerability, we began sharing our feelings—each story layered with grief, frustration, and the longing for connection. My sister spoke of her anger, the way it made her feel free yet bound by sadness. My brother talked about the pressure he felt to carry the family forward while grappling with his own feelings of loss. And mom shared the loneliness of navigating widowhood, the sheer weight of responsibility that left her feeling overwhelmed.

As the world outside our walls continued to shift and grow, I found strength in my family's bond amidst life's complexities. Together, we grappled with the pain of our reality while fostering hope for a brighter future. Each day laid the foundation for resilience—a resilience that would not only withstand the currents of our present but would surge toward the promise of tomorrow, embedding strength and love within every fiber of our shared journey.

My mother was not just a survivor; she was a builder in every sense of the word. Determined to secure a better life for our family, she decided that the very foundations of our home should reflect the resilience and strength of our journey thus far. With the spark of hope ignited by the promises made during her meeting with the town superintendent, she set out on a project that would showcase her tenacity: building our dream home from the ground up.

With little savings and limited resources, my mother approached Mr. Jackson, a local businessman known for his generosity and access to building supplies. He was a fixture in the community, a kind-hearted man who understood the struggles faced by families like ours. Over the years, he had fostered relationships with many people, and mom was determined to make that connection work to our advantage.

One sun-drenched morning, I accompanied mom to Mr. Jackson's supply yard. The vast lot was filled with lumber, bricks, and bags of cement—a treasure trove for those daring enough to dream beyond their current circumstances. My heart raced with anticipation as we approached Mr. Jackson, who was leaning against a stack of timber, his warm smile instantly putting us at ease.

"Ms. Mattie, what brings you two here today?" he greeted, his voice resonating with genuine warmth. My mother didn't waste time; she laid out her vision, her dream of building a sturdy home for her children—a space filled with love, laughter, and memories.

Mr. Jackson listened intently, nodding along as my mother spoke of her intentions. "I want to create a sanctuary for my children," she explained, her eyes sparkling with determination. "A place where they can flourish, be safe, and have room to grow."

"Well, you've come to the right place," Mr. Jackson replied, his tone both supportive and reassuring. "I can help you get started. I'll give you a fair deal on the materials you'll need." My heart surged with gratitude at his willingness to assist, relieved that we had found an ally in our corner.

Over the next few weeks, my mother orchestrated the logistics of our project, planning diligently for the materials we would need—from timber and nails to roofing and cement. I watched as my mother transformed into a force of nature, calculating how much we could carry and anticipating the work ahead.

The journey wasn't without challenges, however. Each day brought its own hurdles: the transportation of supplies, finding helpers in the community, and managing the workload alongside her domestic responsibilities. I admired how my mother faced adversity with unwavering resolve. She frequently returned to the yard, hauling loads of supplies with me and my siblings by her side, our hands small but filled with determination to assist in the construction of our future.

As we began the groundwork, my brother took on the role of overseer, guiding and helping coordinate small tasks. Together, we mixed cement, measured wood, and began laying the foundation. Our home took shape with every passing day—walls rising up, framed windows that stood like open eyes to the world, and a roof that sheltered our aspirations.

The community took notice of my mother's ambitious project. Inspired by her leadership and resilience, neighbors began to lend a hand, attracted by the unifying spirit she invoked in others. Men and women from the area brought tools, offered their skills in construction, or simply provided a hearty meal to keep the workers energized. Their assistance became a powerful testament to the strength found in the community.

As walls went up and the structure began to take form, our home was fast becoming a symbol not just of material success but of hope and perseverance. It was a place that came to life with laughter, where my mother held family meetings to discuss visions for the future, blending practicality with dreams that painted the air with palpable energy.

In the evenings, when the sun dipped below the horizon, turning the sky to hues of orange and pink, my siblings and I would gather together as mom shared stories in the glow of the fading light. She recounted her own childhood and the tales of resilience shared by her family, helping us understand the legacy of strength that enveloped us.

"Every nail driven in this house," she would say softly, "this a promise to you all—to protect you, to nurture you, and to cultivate a space where you can chase your dreams." In those moments, I felt the weight of my mother's love surrounding us like a warm embrace.

As the final pieces of our home fell into place, I saw not just bricks and mortar but the spirit of our family interwoven with every aspect of the structure. This home was a manifestation of our struggles, a beacon of hope in a world that often lingered in shadows. We were reclaiming our space, our story, and our future—a home where we could thrive despite the challenges surrounding us.

When the day came to celebrate the completion of our home, the modest gathering of friends, family, and neighbors marked a historical moment in our lives. We stood together, our spirits alight with joy and pride, a testament to our collective perseverance. My mother beamed as she looked around, the culmination of her dreams surrounded by the love of her children and the support of a community united by purpose.

In that moment, we knew we were not just building a house but crafting a foundation for a better life, fortified by love, resilience, and hope for the future. And as I gazed at the sturdy walls rising against the sky, I felt the strength of my mother's spirit propelling us forward, ready to embrace whatever challenges lay ahead with unyielding determination.

Despite our newfound home—built with love, sweat, and the unwavering support of our community—life continued to challenge my family and me. Just as we began to settle into our new space and dreams, my mother's health took a turn for the worse. The illness that had previously lingered like a heavy cloud began to overshadow our lives once more, dragging my siblings and me back into the turmoil of uncertainty.

There were nights when mom would cough, painful and guttural, her frail body succumbing to the relentless tides of her illness. I would sit up in bed, heart racing as I listened to those sounds echoing through our home. The joyous laughter that had filled our walls was often replaced by quiet sobs of worry.

Eventually, mom's condition grew severe enough that she required hospitalization again. It was a difficult decision, but the weight of her suffering forced her to seek help. I could see the exhaustion etched onto her face, and I felt a mix of fear and love as I watched her bravely agree to admit herself once more.

With mom in the hospital, my brother, sister, and I faced new challenges. We were uprooted from our home, forced to shuffle between the homes of relatives and friends. While we received kindness from family and community members, moving in and out of different homes left us feeling unsettled, as though we were in a state of limbo.

During this transitional period, I felt the sting of loss more acutely. Every time I left one home to move to another, it felt like losing a piece of my stability. I was often crammed into homes already bustling with activity, where families were struggling to make ends meet themselves. I took note of the myriad circumstances at each stop—a living room cluttered with toys, a kitchen bustling with cooks, laughter echoing in shared spaces—but none replaced the feeling of security I once found within the walls of my own home.

At times, my siblings would act out, frustration and confusion bubbling beneath the surface. My sister, struggling with her own grief, would assert her independence by clashing with relatives over chores or expectations. "I don't need to be told what to do!" she would shout, storming off to her room in defiance, the echo of our dad's absence looming large over our interactions.

Caught in the emotional tumult, I sought to mediate, to bring some semblance of peace to our disjointed lives. But I also felt the weight of those struggles consuming my own spirit. The heavy emotions that pulsed through our family felt exhausting—an overwhelming tide that seemed determined to push me under.

During one particularly rough evening at my aunt's house, I gathered my siblings and retreated to a quiet corner of the yard, away from the bustling kitchen filled with chatter. "We have to stick together," I told them softly, my voice firm but gentle. "Mom needs us to be strong. We can't let this break us." My brother nodded gravely, though his eyes betrayed the turbulence he felt inside. "But it's not fair," he said, his voice cracking slightly. "Why does it always have to be us? Why can't we just have a normal life?"I understood his pain—I felt it too—each word resonating within my heart. "I know," I whispered, "but we have each other. That has to count for something. Mom fought for us, and we need to keep fighting for her—and for ourselves." As days turned into weeks, my mother remained hospitalized, leaving us to find ways to cope and adapt to our new reality. I began to take on more responsibility, "I helped my siblings cope with their unfamiliar emotions while also assisting in the homes we stayed in. Through the chaos, I came to appreciate the beauty of community support, where each shared meal, kind word, and thoughtful gesture deepened the connections between us."

"With every passing visit to the hospital, I saw mom grow weaker, yet the fire in her eyes had not dimmed. Each time she cracked a smile and whispered words of encouragement, I found myself anchored by her resilience. "You are stronger than you know, my love," she would say, pushing back against the pain, reminding me of the power of love and fortitude and sensed that my mother was fighting not only for her own life but also for the dreams she had fostered for my siblings and me, as well as the community we belonged to. Through her battles, I felt a spark of determination return to my own spirit. Perseverance became our family mantra, expressed in hushed tones during evening prayers.

As the days turned into an endless cycle of hope and uncertainty, I discovered comfort in small routines. I began to take walks with my siblings, visiting the nearby park when we could, and finding solace in the freshness of nature. We played games and shared laughter, free from the pressures of daily life, even if just for a moment. Those small pockets of joy reaffirmed the love we held for each other, weaving a fabric of connection that no turmoil could tear apart."

Ultimately, my mother's health began to show slight signs of improvement, and she eventually made her way back home. The day she returned was one filled with relief and gratitude that enveloped us all. Though we would still face the shadows of illness and uncertainty, we understood now that resilience lived within us—to make it as solid and impactful as the walls of our home we built together.

Slowly, we settled back into a rhythm, once again finding honor in our routines. Mom, though still fragile, took the lead, instilling hope in our hearts. She assured us that together, we would navigate whatever challenges lay ahead, fortified by love, shared stories, and a collective commitment to one another.

As we rebuilt our lives yet again—this time not just with bricks and mortar, but with the tenacity of spirit that defined us—I began to envision a future where we could thrive despite our struggles. We were weaving our way through adversity with strength and love, forming a new legacy of resilience that would define our home, our community, and our very existence.

As I transitioned into my teenage years, life continued to present challenges that tested my resilience and spirit. Mom's health fluctuated, at times necessitating extended stays in the hospital for treatments that affected not only her physical body but also her mental well-being. The distance from home weighed heavily on my heart, knowing that my mother's battle extended beyond the confines of her physical illness and into the depths of mental and emotional turmoil.

The hospital mom was admitted to was known for treating patients grappling with severe mental health challenges, including depression and anxiety. While I understood the importance of my mother receiving the care she needed, the distance felt insurmountable. The separation often left me both worried and longing for the moments we had once spent together.

During this critical period, my auntie—an embodiment of unwavering faith and devotion—stepped in to care for my siblings and me. Auntie would come to our home regularly, bringing warmth, comfort, and a strong spiritual presence that anchored me amidst the chaos. With a heart full of hope and a steadfast belief in God's power, Auntie shared the importance of prayer, emphasizing that faith could guide us through even the darkest of days.

I watched with admiration as Auntie devoted hours each week, transforming our living space into a sanctuary of prayer and reflection. We would gather in the living room, the soft light of the evening casting gentle shadows across the walls, and Auntie would lead us in prayer—her voice a soothing melody that filled the room with messages of hope.

Remember, children," Auntie would say, her eyes shining with faith, "God hears our prayers. He is always with us, especially when we feel distant or alone. We must trust in His plan." This sense of spiritual foundation became a lifeline for me, bridging the gap created by my mother's absence.

Inspired by these experiences, I began to cultivate my own connection to faith. I sought solace in reading scripture, finding passages that resonated with my struggles and anchored me in moments of uncertainty. The stories of resilience and love found in the tales of biblical figures became a source of strength; I learned to lean on that strength when the weight of worry threatened to overwhelm me.

In my mother's absence, I felt the pull to take on the nurturing role once held so firmly by both my mother and my auntie. I became the caretaker of my siblings, balancing schoolwork and household chores with the responsibilities of guiding my brother and sister through their own feelings of loss and uncertainty. Each night, I tucked them into bed, sharing stories and quiet reassurances. "Mom will be back soon," I would promise, though I too felt the tremors of doubt beneath the surface.

With every passing week, I reflected on the legacies of the remarkable women in my life—my mother, known for her tireless work ethic and dedication to family; and my auntie, a fierce believer whose prayers acted as a protective shield around us. I aspired to embody their strength, reminding myself that resilience was not a trait I would carry alone but a gift passed down through generations.

The community began to notice the shift in me, my spirit embodying the tenacity of the women who had shaped me. I began participating in community activities, channeling my energy into positive outlets—engaging with local events and extending kindness to neighbors in need. I believed in faith and hope, sharing them at gatherings organized by my auntie and other community members.

My own journey of growth became intertwined with my mother's legacy. In each prayer, in every kind act, I honored the women who had shaped my life, ensuring that their spirits would continue to guide me. "I am a product of resilience," I reminded myself, each day determined to rise to the occasion, despite the challenges we faced.

Then, one fateful day, I received a call from the hospital—a call that stirred a whirlwind of emotions. My mother had shown signs of progress and had been expressing a desire to return home. Waves of hope washed over me, intertwined with trepidation about what adjustments lay ahead. Would my mother be the same? How would I navigate this new chapter filled with the weight of mental health struggles?

When my mother finally came home, even after the hospital's interventions, she seemed a shadow of the vibrant woman I remembered. Her eyes, once filled with dreams and laughter, held a far-off gaze, one that spoke volumes of the battles she had faced. But as soon as she stepped inside, I enveloped her in an embrace, feeling the warmth of her spirit, knowing that home was where healing began.

With Auntie's guidance and the strength cultivated from adversity, I embraced mom's return with grace and patience. Together, we began to navigate the complexities of healing, employing practices of self-care and community—our home once again becoming a sanctuary, not only for us but for all those seeking solace.

In that moment of reunification, I could feel the dual legacy of mom and auntie intertwined within me. Inspired, I took on a conscious role as an advocate for mental health awareness, speaking openly about our family's experiences in our community. I sought to create a dialogue around mental health, ensuring that no one felt isolated or alone in their struggles—solidifying my commitment to carry forward the lessons I learned from the amazing women in my life.

As our journey continued, I discovered that while the road may not always be smooth, it was a road worth walking together, fortified by love and faith. With each step forward, we continued to build a life filled with hope, resilience, and the spirit of the remarkable women who had shaped us, paving the way for a future we would create—not alone, but together, unabashedly united in our strength.

As my family and I settled into this new chapter of our lives, we found ourselves surrounded by the vibrant pulse of Black culture in the South—a culture rich with history, creativity, and an unwavering spirit of resilience. The community around us was alive with the sounds of jazz, blues, and gospel music, each note echoing the struggles and triumphs of those who came before us. Musicians filled local bars and street corners, their melodies serving as both a celebration of our heritage and a poignant reminder of the battles fought for equality.

I became increasingly aware of the importance of this cultural tapestry, understanding that music, art, and literature intertwined with our narratives of perseverance. The songs performed by local artists told stories of pain and joy, weaving messages of hope and resistance into each lyric. Every performance seemed to echo the hearts of our ancestors, grounding me in the legacy of those who had worked, strived, and carved a place for themselves amid the oppression.

The allure of music also ignited a flame within me. I began attending local events where musicians gathered to share their talents and stories. I felt a deep connection to the rhythms, melodies, and emotions swirling around me—a yearning to capture my own thoughts and experiences through words and songs. With my notebook in hand, I jotted down ideas and verses inspired by the performances, drawing from the truth of my life and the rich narratives unfolding around me.

Not far from where we lived, in the heart of Jackson, a collective of civil rights leaders rose, committed to fighting against the injustices that permeated our society. Figures like Medgar Evers and many others began organizing marches, sit-ins, and community meetings, igniting a powerful movement that echoed through the streets. I found myself inspired by their courage and resilience, watching as they paved a path toward justice for future generations.

My mother, despite still grappling with her own struggles, became increasingly involved in these discussions, attending meetings alongside Auntie and encouraging us to learn and speak out about the importance of civil rights. "You must know your history, sweet child. It's essential for us to remember where we came from, so we can continue to march forward," my mother urged, her voice encouraging and strong.

The conversations at home often turned to these leaders and the movements they were igniting, as the air crackled with passion and determination. Inspired, I began attending local gatherings, where community members shared their stories and experiences. At these meetings, I met individuals whose struggles mirrored my own family's journey—those determined to reclaim their voices, to stand together against discrimination, and to forge a future of equality.

I took to heart the responsibilities that came with this newfound knowledge and inspiration. I stumbled upon opportunities to join youth organizations focused on civil rights advocacy, feeling invigorated as I networked with fellow youth passionate about making a difference. We organized events, rallies, and discussions about the importance of social justice, mobilizing our peers to raise awareness of the issues plaguing our communities.

Inspired by stories of historical figures like Rosa Parks, Harriet Tubman, and Malcolm X, I crafted my own identity within this movement, deciding to speak at events and share my experiences. My heartfelt stories resonated deeply with my peers, articulating the frustrations, hopes, and dreams of young Black individuals grappling with the realities of discrimination.

As my voice began to gain traction, I collaborated with local artists and musicians to create platforms that uplifted our community's narratives. The combination of my story with music became a driving force, merging my love for both art forms to create powerful performances that expressed our collective experiences. Concerts turned into communal gatherings, fostering a sense of unity and belonging among those fighting for their rights.

Furthermore, my commitment fueled a spirit of togetherness that transcended individuals' struggles—members from various backgrounds began joining forces, crafting a coalition rooted in love for humanity. A chorus of voices emerged loud and clear, echoing the desire for change, for justice, and for recognition across the South.

Through this tireless work, I found the purpose in my own story. Determined to honor my family's legacy and the countless individuals who fought for civil rights, I poured my heart into my art, infusing my words with power and empathy. By drawing alliances, collaborating with my community, and forging bonds among artists, I contributed to a movement that celebrated our culture and continued to challenge societal norms—all while nourishing my own spirit after so much tragedy.

As my mother started to regain strength, she witnessed me stepping into my own power. "I'm proud of you, my daughter. You're carrying the torch forward," she said one evening, tears glimmering in her eyes. I felt emboldened by her acknowledgment, understanding that I was part of something larger than myself—an unyielding force fueled by history, hope, and the relentless pursuit of justice.

The decades rolled on, and while the struggles persisted, so did the spirit of resilience in our community. I stood tall, illuminated by the strength of the women before me and the cultural heritage that held me up, proudly embodying the fight while pouring my essence into every word sung, every poem recited, and every dream cherished.

In the heart of the South, where adversity was met with unyielding strength, my community and I continued to thrive. The stories of our people burgeoned—a musical testament to our triumphs, woven together by a collective heartbeat that promised brighter tomorrows. Together, we fought, we celebrated, and we thrived, forever etching our own powerful legacy into the fabric of history.

As I entered young adulthood, I found myself navigating newfound independence, balancing my activism with my aspirations. My passion continued to flourish, and I began to dream about a future filled with love, purpose, and family. It was during this pivotal time in my life that I met a man who would change everything—a man who walked through the doors of the restaurant where I worked.

The restaurant where I worked was a lively establishment, a hub of community activity situated in a vibrant part of Jackson. It was not only a place to dine but also a meeting ground for friends and families, a melting pot filled with laughter, stories, and the rich aroma of Southern cuisine. I had taken a job there to help support my family while also pursuing my passions, hoping to save money for my future endeavors.

His name was Curtis, and the moment I first laid eyes on him, I felt a spark—a familiar sense of belonging, as if my heart recognized his presence in a way that transcended the ordinary. The smile he flashed when he stepped behind the counter to introduce himself was warm and genuine, and his laughter blended effortlessly with the bustling atmosphere around us. He was charming, with a lightness about him that drew people in, and I found myself enchanted.

As we began to work together, our connection deepened. Curtis, with his easy charm and caring nature, quickly became a ray of sunshine in my busy days. He had a knack for storytelling, weaving tales that captivated our coworkers during lull periods between shifts. I admired his passion for life.

The more time I spent with Curtis, the more I discovered how much we had in common. We both believed in the power of community and shared dreams of making a difference in the world. Our late-night discussions about social justice, music, and family drew us closer—an unspoken bond forming as we found solace and strength in each other's words.

From that day on, our friendship blossomed into something deeper. We began to explore the beauty of our city together, strolling through the parks, attending community events, and supporting each other's dreams.

After several months of laughter, shared dreams, and soul-baring conversations, Curtis finally mustered the courage to take our relationship to the next level. One evening, as we walked under the canopy of stars, he paused in front of a picturesque view of Jackson's skyline. With a tender gaze, he took my hands in his and spoke softly, "You've brought so much joy into my life. I can't imagine a future without you. Will you be my partner in this journey?"

In that moment, with my heart racing, I realized I had found a love that matched my own passion for life—a partner who would stand by me through the ups and downs. "Yes," I breathed, my eyes shimmering with tears of joy. "I want that too."

Our relationship deepened over the years, evolving into a beautiful partnership filled with shared goals. As we navigated the complexities of adulthood, we supported each other in both our personal and professional ambitions.

Years later, sitting side by side in our living room, I reflected on the journey that had brought us to this moment. The walls of our home were adorned with reminders of our shared dreams—framed photographs, paintings from local artists, and lyrics written on scraps of paper, all echoing the support of our community. I smiled, filled with gratitude for the journey we had shared—the laughter, the love, the hopes, and the dreams, all woven into the fabric of our lives. Together, we faced whatever challenges lay ahead, our bond fortified by the richness of our experiences and the indelible spirit of our community lingering in every beat of our shared story. In the heart of Jackson, I had found not just love, but a partner to navigate the symphony of life—a melody we would compose together, reverberating through the years.

As Curtis and I carved out a loving life together in Jackson, the atmosphere across the South began to shift dramatically. Just as we had found the flourishing community and support that nourished our dreams, a shadow loomed on the horizon—the rise of the Ku Klux Klan. Their presence started to infiltrate the town, reminding me and those around us of the deeply rooted hatred that remained pervasive, casting an ominous pall over the progress we had fought for.

In the wake of the emerging Klan activity, the community's sense of security began to unravel. Reports surfaced of rallies and demonstrations, not just in Jackson but throughout the surrounding areas. The Klan thrived on fear, and they sought to intimidate Black families and those sympathetic to civil rights causes. I could feel the tension in the air—a mix of dread and resolve as conversations about safety and unity circulated through our community.

Curtis and I would often sit late into the night, discussing the changes unfolding around us. "This isn't just about us anymore," Curtis said one evening, his brow furrowed in concern. "It's about our community—our friends, our families. We need to stand together." I nodded in agreement, tears brimming in my eyes. The spirit of love and resilience we had cultivated felt threatened in ways that were deeply unsettling.

The Klan, emboldened by newfound confidence, began to openly target local leaders who advocated for civil rights, and soon, their actions turned violent. Attacks on homes and businesses became headlines in the local news; fear was palpable. My heart raced each time I heard murmurs of Klan members being spotted nearby. This was a war that extended beyond the walls of our home—it threatened the very fabric of our lives.

The summer days stretched long as the community rallied together, each voice adding to the chorus of change. We held prayer meetings, community forums, and peaceful demonstrations, ensuring that our spirits remained unbroken. Even when faced with violent acts from the Klan, families banded together, offering protection, support, and strength to one another, reinforcing the belief that we would not cower or retreat.

Together, Curtis and I became a force for change, echoing the songs, stories, and struggles of those who had walked the path before us. We believed in our community and its ability to rise above the darkness that loomed, nurturing a flame of hope that burned brightly even in the most turbulent of times.

As summer faded into autumn, the fight against the Klan persisted, but so did the determination of those of us who refused to let hatred define our futures. With love as our foundation, we forged ahead, unwavering in our quest for justice and equality.

The legacy of our ancestors and the strength of our community propelled us forward, illuminating a path of hope, resilience, and relentless strength against the tide of adversity.

As the seasons unfolded in Jackson, filled with both trials and triumphs against the backdrop of rising tensions and profound love, Curtis and I embraced new chapters in our lives—chapters that would weave our stories deeper into the tapestry of family, resilience, and joy.

Our family grew, and although the rise of the Klan and the unease within our neighborhood remained ever-present, Curtis and I resolved that our children would know the strength of our community. We participated in family-friendly events that normalized conversations about history and justice, wanting our children to understand the significance of their heritage, the sacrifices their ancestors made, and the ongoing fight for equality.

One evening, with the sunset casting a golden glow across the park, I took to the stage alongside Curtis and our children. It was a night meant not only to celebrate our heritage but to show the strength we had cultivated amidst adversity. I spoke about love, the strength of family, and the legacy we were creating for our children—a legacy defined by hope and thriving resistance against hate. "Never forget," I told the crowd, my voice ringing with passion, "we are the torchbearers of change. Together, we can create a future where our children can dance and sing without fear. They represent our dreams, our joy, our relentless spirit."

In time, Curtis and I would see our family grow to include more children, each carrying the essence of their parents and the legacy of love that would inspire future generations. We fostered a home that was a blend of laughter and music, stories of heroes and dreams of change—a safe haven where our children could learn the power of love and community while embracing their heritage wholeheartedly.

As we celebrated the lives we created, Curtis and I continued to embody perseverance. We formed a family legacy filled with hope, unity, strength, and unwavering laughter, ensuring that our children would know the power of their roots, the richness of their culture, and the beauty of embracing life with love in their hearts. Together, we crafted not only a household but a movement—a testament to the enduring spirit of our family and community.

As I settled into the rhythm of family life, I came to realize that raising children amidst the complexities of our world was no easy feat. The joys of motherhood were often punctuated by the weight of responsibilities that seemed to pile up around me. When I married Curtis at the tender age of 19, I had envisioned a life filled with love and laughter, but the challenges of adulthood quickly revealed themselves.

Balancing the demands of work and motherhood proved to be a constant struggle. I worked tirelessly both at home and at my job at the restaurant, often juggling shifts that left me feeling exhausted. Each day was a delicate balancing act, where I found myself torn between my responsibilities to my children, my work, and my extended family.

One of the additional challenges stemmed from the need to support my sister, who was also navigating life as a parent. With my own children in need of guidance and care, I often felt the burden of helping my sister, ensuring that my nieces and nephews felt love and support. The drive to help family was ingrained in me, a value instilled by my own upbringing, but at times, it felt overwhelming.

I would spend time with my sister, caring for the children while also trying to provide emotional support. I felt a deep sense of responsibility, knowing that my sister was facing her struggles. There were weekends where my own children would play freely, while I organized playdates for my nieces and nephews, ensuring that everyone was entertained and cared for. "I wish things were easier for you," I often told my sister during our late-night talks, my voice soft yet steady. "But we are family, and we'll always figure it out together."

During these moments, I felt a rush of love and an unshakeable determination to uplift those around me. Yet, within, I grappled with feelings of exhaustion and weariness—longing for a moment to catch my breath. As I tucked my children into bed each night, I would lay awake, contemplating the day's events, the responsibilities heavy on my heart.

Adding to my plate was my commitment to supporting my mother, who, despite her battles with health, remained a pillar in our family. I would often help her with errands, doctors' appointments, and household tasks. These responsibilities, while fulfilling, at times felt burdensome. "Mom, you've done so much for us," I would say, my gaze affectionate yet tinged with worry as I held her hand. "You shouldn't have to worry about everything. Just focus on getting well."

My mother would smile softly and squeeze my hand in return, an unspoken love shared between us. Yet, I could not shake the feeling that I was being pulled in countless directions, my heart divided among those I loved. Despite it all, I found strength in my marriage to Curtis. He became my anchor—a steadfast partner who was unwavering in his support. Together, we learned to navigate the complexities of our lives, organizing our schedules to ensure we could be there for our children and each other. Curtis stepped in whenever he could, sharing in parenting duties and providing a comforting presence during difficult days.

"Let's take it one day at a time," he would remind me, his voice warm and reassuring. "We're in this together." He encouraged me to pursue my passions, reminding me that my voice was essential—not just in our family but in the community work we were dedicated to. Slowly, I learned to carve out small pockets of time for myself—moments where I could write or reflect, allowing my creativity to flow as I documented the ups and downs of our lives.

Our evenings would often find us sitting together after the children had gone to bed. These moments of creativity allowed me to process my feelings, providing an emotional outlet that renewed my resolve. Despite the myriad challenges, I remained connected to my purpose—my commitment to my family drove me forward. I began to appreciate the moments of laughter, the stories shared at the dinner table, and the resilience that flourished amid adversity. Through the chaos, I learned that love was the strongest glue, binding our family together in the face of life's trials.

As we continued raising our children, I understood that while life would pose challenges—whether it was helping my sister, supporting my mother, or managing my duties as a wife and mother—we would face them together, united in our mission to create a home filled with love and hope.

In the midst of a complex life, I realized that every challenge was also an opportunity for growth. I found strength in my family, in the bonds we shared, and in the knowledge that love could weather any storm. Together with Curtis, we would carve out a future—not just for ourselves but for the children we were raising, honoring our legacy and ensuring that the light of our love would continue to shine brightly.

As the tumultuous atmosphere in Jackson intensified with the growing presence of the Ku Klux Klan, I felt the strain of the societal upheaval weighing heavily on me and my community. The civil rights movement, which had ignited hope and dreams of a more equitable society, was being challenged by the resurgence of hate, casting a shadow over the progress that had been made.

Life was growing increasingly difficult, balancing my family responsibilities while trying to stay informed and involved in the ongoing struggles for justice. The streets of Jackson, which had once felt familiar and safe, now buzzed with tension, as activist voices clashed with those seeking to sow discord and fear. News of violence against peaceful demonstrators and community leaders rattled me, making me acutely aware of the risks associated with standing up for what was right.

One bright afternoon while returning from the local store, my mind filled with thoughts of my children and the mounting pressures I faced, I found myself on Farish Street. It was a street that had witnessed countless conversations about hope and change—a place where activism thrived amid community bonds. As I walked, lost in reflection, I was unexpectedly approached by a familiar figure: Medgar Evers, a prominent civil rights leader and Mississippi's state field secretary for the NAACP. He stopped me and asked, "Are you registered to vote?" His question seemed to echo the urgent calls for action in the community—a question that bore significant weight during such uncertain times.

Taken aback for a moment, I felt a mix of emotions surge through me. The right to vote was a fundamental pillar of the civil rights movement, a right fought for by so many who came before me. However, I also understood the subtle fear that lingered in the air, knowing that the act of registering—and especially voting—could expose one to the very real threat of violence from groups like the Klan."I've been meaning to," I admitted, a hint of uncertainty in my tone. "But with everything going on… it's hard to know what to prioritize."

Medgar nodded, his expression serious but understanding. "I get that; it's a challenging time for all of us. But registering is crucial. It's our way to fight against the tide of hate that seeks to silence us. Your voice matters, Hyrtecene." I felt a sense of fire rekindle within me. "You're right. It's just scary, you know? I want to protect my children, and I worry about the repercussions."The concern in my voice did not go unnoticed. Medgar stepped closer, bringing a sense of solidarity to the moment. "I understand your fears, deeply. But remember, we can't let fear dictate our actions. Every day, people are risking everything for the freedom we deserve. If we want our children to grow up in a better world, we must seize every opportunity to uplift our voices."

Our conversation stirred something within me—a resolve to take action despite the challenges looming over me and my community. I had grown accustomed to standing on the sidelines, helping others but hesitating to claim my own place in this fight.

"I will register," I declared, my voice emboldened. "My children deserve a future free from fear and hatred." Medgar smiled, a gleam of pride shining in his eyes. "That's the spirit. You're stronger than you know, Hyrtecene. Let's not forget—every time we stand together, we galvanize others to do the same. I'll be around to support you and can help get you to the registration office."

As we parted ways, I felt a renewed sense of purpose pulsing within me. Medgar's words resonate in my heart, reminding me that my involvement mattered. I returned home, invigorated by the encounter, determined to discuss with Curtis the importance of community engagement and the steps we could take as a family.

That evening, I gathered my children and Curtis around the table, sharing my conversation with Medgar and the significance of registering to vote. I watched as Curtis nodded thoughtfully, and the children listened, their eyes wide with curiosity."I want us to be part of this movement," Curtis stated firmly, his eyes filled with pride. "If we want to see change, we have to stand together as a family. We can't let fear silence us."

And with that, we began to explore the process of voter registration as a family, teaching our children about civic responsibility and the power of community engagement. I felt a weight lift as we gathered around the kitchen table, searching together for local voter registration resources, strengthening our bond through shared purpose.

Though the challenges that lay ahead remained daunting, I embraced the idea that together, we could face any adversity. The spirit of activism coursed through our family like a lifeblood, binding us closer while fortifying our resolve to seek justice.

As the fight for civil rights continued, I felt empowered to take my place in the movement, not just for my community but also for my children—ensuring they would inherit a legacy defined by courage, love, and an unwavering commitment to standing against hate.

The oppressive atmosphere in Jackson began to reach a boiling point as the civil rights movement faced fierce resistance from those determined to maintain the status quo. The outrage against unjust laws, systemic racism, and the brutal acts of violence perpetrated by groups like the Ku Klux Klan had ignited a flame of anger and determination within our Black community. I could feel the pulse of change reverberating through the streets, but it also bore the weight of deep fear and sorrow.

As I turned on the news one evening, my heart sank at the reports of riots breaking out across the city—a reaction to the latest episode of violence inflicted upon an innocent Black man. The sight of angry faces, families demanding justice, and the chaotic atmosphere of protest sent a chill down my spine. I knew these riots were born from desperation. Hopelessness grappled with the demand for justice in a society where lynching and hatred had taken root.

I felt the knot in my stomach twist tighter as the events unfolded, understanding that the anger I felt was echoed throughout my community. This was not a distant issue; it was a stark reminder of the challenges we faced each day. It was personal. Friends and neighbors became embroiled in the growing tension as we gathered to advocate for our rights.

One evening, I stepped outside to find the streets lit up by the flickering glow of torches and the muffled sound of chants rising in the distance. "No justice, no peace" echoed like a resolute battle cry, a collective voice demanding to be seen and heard. The sight brought forth a myriad of emotions—pride, fear, anger, and a deep sense of urgency.

Determined to understand what was happening, I walked towards the gathering. I was met by a diverse crowd of people—old and young, men and women—all united by a singular mission. They sought to bring awareness to the injustices surrounding us, to confront the brutal reality we lived in, and to demand accountability for the lives lost to senseless violence. The air was thick with a turbulent energy—one that indicated moments of uplift and sorrow, as we shared stories of loved ones who had faced unimaginable terror.

However, the evening quickly turned chaotic as counter-protesters arrived, attempting to silence the voices we sought to uphold. Tension escalated, and I watched as bottles flew and people scrambled to find safety. The chaos spiraled, and before long, I found myself swept into the frantic crowd, my heart racing with fear.

"Stay together!" I shouted to a group nearby, feeling the gravity of the moment. I recognized many faces—friends, fellow activists—people I knew were there to fight for justice but were suddenly confronted by a violent backlash. The rioters and counter-protesters clashed as shouts of anger rang out from every direction, revealing the stark divides that still tore at the heart of our community.

Overwhelmed by the sheer weight of the reality we faced, I felt tears welling in my eyes. I thought of my children and the future I wanted to protect for them. It was imperative to find a way to ensure they would grow up in a world where they could walk freely without fear, but how could we ever achieve that amid these relentless cycles of violence and hatred?

I turned back toward the direction of home, instincts propelling me forward, knowing I had to return to my children. As I walked, I could hear the distant echoes of sirens, the anguish of the night's turmoil rising even higher, intensifying like a wildfire out of control. When I arrived home, I found Curtis seated at the kitchen table, eyes heavy with worry. "I was hoping you wouldn't go out there," he said, his tone urgent but filled with understanding. "The streets aren't safe right now. There's a lot of anger, and they're retaliating against anyone who stands up for their rights." I nodded, the gravity of my experiences weighing down on me. "It's terrifying, Curtis. But these people are fighting for our lives, for the future of our children. We can't sit back and do nothing."

Curtis leaned closer, determination etched on his face. "I agree, but we have to approach this carefully. We can't afford to lose ourselves or our family in this chaos. We need to channel that anger, that pain, into something positive—something that helps change the narrative instead of escalating violence." My children were still awake, huddled together on the living room floor, alarmed by the distant echoes of unrest outside. I knelt beside them, my heart aching as I looked into their innocent eyes. How could I explain the world they lived in? How could I share the complexities of a fight they didn't yet fully understand?

In that moment of reflection, I realized that my children needed to know about the strength of community, the power of unity, and the importance of standing up for what was right. "Listen, my loves," I began gently, kneeling before them. "The world outside isn't always fair. It's filled with things that can be scary, like injustice and hatred. But remember, we are strong. Together, we can work toward change, and we will always be here to protect one another." My children listened, wide-eyed, as I reminded them that while the world could be filled with darkness, they were the light—shining bright, no matter the challenges they faced.

Over the ensuing weeks, as tensions escalated and the violence continued, Curtis and I remained steadfast in our commitment to fostering hope within our family and community. We began organizing small gatherings, promoting dialogues about civil rights and community dynamics. This became a safe space where community members could share their experiences and feelings about the unrest, offering solace amidst the upheaval that rattled our lives. Together, we worked tirelessly to create educational opportunities for our children and neighbors, encouraging critical discussions about the importance of civic engagement and the fight against systemic racism. We collaborated with other families and activists, channeling the anger from recent riots into positive action—organizing peaceful demonstrations, promoting voter registration drives, and providing platforms for local leaders to speak out against injustice.

As we stood in solidarity through the darkness, I felt a spark of hope ignite within me. Amid the threat of violence and despair, we were determined to ensure our voices were heard, our stories shared—a testament to the resilience of our community. We understood that change wouldn't come easily, but with perseverance and a shared commitment to justice, our efforts could pave the way toward a future defined not by fear but by love and unity. And so, united in our resolve, Curtis, our children, and I continued to shine light into the darkness—persistent in our fight against hatred and unwavering in our belief that peace and justice would someday prevail.

As the decision to leave Mississippi became inevitable in the wake of Medgar Evers' tragic death, Curtis and I faced an emotional crossroads in our lives. With heavy hearts, we knew that we each had to embark on separate paths to ensure a better future for our children. I made the brave choice to journey to New York, driven by the opportunity to take a job my mother had discovered. The bustling energy of the city promised a chance for new beginnings—a fresh start for me and my children. I packed our belongings and gathered the kids, determined to create a safe environment for them amidst the chaos of our past.

Meanwhile, Curtis opted to move to Kalamazoo, Michigan, where he believed he could find work and establish himself. It was a difficult decision for both of us, as we realized that separating, even temporarily, would bring its own set of challenges. Despite the distance, we both understood the necessity of our choices—each committed to the well-being of our family.

The day we departed was filled with bittersweet moments. I embraced Curtis tightly, feeling the weight of uncertainty envelop us. "It's going to be okay," I whispered, even as tears streamed down my cheeks. Curtis nodded, his eyes reflecting a mix of hope and sorrow. "We'll find our way, Hyrtecene. This is just a chapter." With that, we parted ways—me heading to the vibrant streets of New York, and Curtis leaving for Kalamazoo, both determined to make our new lives meaningful for our children.

As I arrived in New York, the city buzzed around me, filled with opportunities and unfamiliarity. I threw myself into my new job, focused on creating a nurturing space for my children while slowly navigating the obstacles of being in an entirely new environment. I found solace in the rhythm of the city, immersing myself in the community around me, eager to forge a sense of belonging. Curtis, on the other hand, settled into his new life in Kalamazoo, looking for work and exploring the local landscape. He often thought of me and our dreams for our children's future. Despite the distance, we communicated frequently, sharing updates about our lives and providing each other with encouragement to keep moving forward.

While living separately was undoubtedly challenging, both Curtis and I knew that we were working toward a shared goal—creating a loving and supportive environment for our children, no matter the distance between us. Each day was a testament to our strength and resilience, as we adapted to our new realities while holding on to the hope that, someday, our paths would converge again, united by the love we had for our family.

As I settled into my new life in Jamaica, Queens, the reality of my separation from Curtis weighed on my heart. We had made the tough decision to part ways for a time, believing it would ultimately benefit our family. Curtis had chosen to stay in Kalamazoo, Michigan, determined to establish himself and find work that would secure a future for us all.

While I thrived in the vibrant atmosphere of New York, Curtis embraced his new reality in Kalamazoo, seeking job opportunities and building connections within the local community. Despite the distance, we maintained regular communication, sharing updates about our lives and offering each other support during difficult times. "It's just a chapter, Hyrtecene," Curtis would reassure me over the phone, his voice filled with unwavering strength. "We're working towards our goals, and we'll find a way to bring our family back together."

Though I missed him dearly, I took comfort in this reminder, recognizing the importance of our individual journeys amid the broader challenges we faced. As I focused on creating a nurturing environment for our children in New York, Curtis poured himself into finding work that aligned with his skills and passions. Our conversations often revolved around hopes for the future—dreams of reuniting as a family and building a life filled with love and security. I filled my days with nurturing our children and fostering community ties, while Curtis actively sought out networks in Kalamazoo, determined to create a stable foundation for our family.

As time passed, my sister joined me in Queens, allowing us to build a familial support system. While the distance from Curtis was challenging, the presence of family brought me a sense of grounding and encouragement. Together, we worked tirelessly to create a sense of home—filled with laughter, love, and a vision for a brighter future. Though our physical separation remained, both Curtis and I stayed committed to our shared goal: to one day reunite our family in a place where we could flourish together. The hope of that reunification fueled our determination, bond, and unwavering trust in the love we held for one another.

In Kalamazoo, Curtis continued to lay down roots, actively seeking opportunities that would allow him to provide for our family. With each passing day, he looked toward the horizon, knowing deep down that the love we had built could withstand any challenge—and that one day, he and I would find our way back into each other's arms, ready to embrace the life we were destined to create together.

As the seasons changed in New York and the vibrant city unfurled its tapestry of opportunities, I embraced my role as a dedicated parent and educator in my children's lives. With all of them enrolled in school, it was a time of growth and exploration for each of us. The hustle and bustle of our daily routines provided a foundation for both learning and bonding, allowing me to actively participate in their educational journeys.

Every morning, I orchestrated the family's busy schedule. I made breakfast for my children, ensuring they started the day with nutritious food to fuel their minds and bodies. As we gathered around the kitchen table, I instilled the importance of communication and reflection. "What are you looking forward to today?" I would ask, encouraging them to share their hopes, dreams, and any fears they might have about the day ahead. I took pride in being involved in their education, knowing that my active participation could profoundly shape their experiences. Whenever the school year kicked off, I volunteered for various activities, from helping in the classroom to organizing events. I became a familiar face to both teachers and parents, showing my children that education extended beyond the walls of a classroom.

Outside of the home, I recognized that education transcended academics. I organized playdates and social gatherings for my children, fostering relationships and connections with peers in the community. These gatherings served not only as fun, but as opportunities for my kids to build friendships and learn the values of teamwork and cooperation. I encouraged my children to be inclusive and empathetic, nurturing their understanding of diversity—the cornerstone of our vibrant neighborhood.

As time went on, the bond between my children and me grew stronger. We laughed together, learned from one another, and faced challenges as a united front. I understood that my role extended beyond that of a parent; I was also a teacher, advocate, and ally who navigated the complexities of both childhood and societal issues alongside them. With each school year that passed, I found myself deeply immersed in not just my children's lives, but in the wider community as well. I collaborated with other parents to form support groups, discussing strategies for addressing challenges faced by our children. Together, we advocated for equitable educational resources in our neighborhood, ensuring that every child had access to the opportunities necessary for success.

In this fast-paced world of New York, I embraced the role of a parent with a fierce resolve. The lessons I learned during our tumultuous journey—the value of resilience, the importance of unity, and the striving for justice—shaped my approach to motherhood and education. As I cultivated a rich, nurturing environment for my children, I understood that I was not just raising individuals; I was laying the groundwork for a generation committed to fostering change and advocating for a better future. Through laughter and challenges, I knew that my family was a testament to the power of love, education, and community. In the heart of Queens, each day brought new opportunities for growth and connection, and as we moved forward, I remained ever vigilant in my mission to guide my children toward a future defined by hope, courage, and an unwavering commitment to justice.

The Move to Brooklyn

The bustle of life in Brooklyn, marked by lively streets, parks, and cultural events, allowed my children to explore and engage with a broader world. We often spent weekends at local fairs, visiting museums, and participating in neighborhood festivities, providing them with experiences that celebrated their diverse backgrounds.

During this time, I began working at P.S. 182 as a teacher's assistant. The position was a perfect fit for me, allowing me to intertwine my passions for education and community. I was thrilled to be part of a vibrant school that reflected the mosaic of cultures present in Brooklyn. Each day brought new experiences and challenges as I engaged with a classroom full of diverse children, giving me a deeper understanding of their needs and aspirations.

At P.S. 182, my role went beyond supporting the teacher; I became an advocate for the children. Recognizing the potential within each student, I dedicated myself to fostering an inclusive environment where every child felt valued. I brought my own experiences of resilience and cultural appreciation into the classroom, igniting curiosity and a love for learning in my students. In my interactions with the children, I often intertwined lessons about history, culture, and the importance of empathy with engaging activities. I organized multicultural events that celebrated the rich backgrounds of my students, inviting families to share their traditions, food, and stories. These gatherings not only brought the community together but taught the children about belonging and the beauty of diversity.

As a mother, I was also committed to instilling similar values in my own children. I encouraged them to embrace their multifaceted identities and to respect and appreciate the differences in those around them. Whether it was sharing stories about our lineage or exploring various cultural traditions, I emphasized that their backgrounds were not just parts of their identities; they were sources of strength. Despite the busyness of my life, I managed to balance my roles as a mother and educator. The love and dedication I poured into my family also translated seamlessly into my work at P.S. 182. I found camaraderie among the faculty, who recognized my efforts and passion for fostering a nurturing and dynamic learning environment.

As a family, we continued to engage in community activities, finding ways to give back and support those around us. My voice resonated not only in my classroom but also within the larger community, advocating for the needs and rights of children and families—an extension of the lessons learned throughout my journey.

In Brooklyn, I flourished as both a mother and educator, committed to uplifting my family and my community. The challenges we had faced became the backdrop for our resilience, and the love we built was the foundation of our new life. With every school day at P.S. 182, every story shared at home, and every cultural celebration embraced, I continued to champion the values of love, education, and unity that would guide our family for generations to come.

My journey through Brooklyn continued to unfold beautifully as I embraced my role at P.S. 182. The vibrant school community became a second home for me, filled with laughter, learning, and an abundance of opportunities to make a difference in children's lives. The experiences I gained there inspired me to think about my own educational aspirations—dreams that had once seemed distant during my tumultuous times in the South.

When I learned that the Board of Education offered a program that would cover my college tuition in exchange for my continued service as a teacher's assistant, I felt a surge of hope and excitement. This was an opportunity I had always dreamed of—pursuing higher education and furthering my ambitions in teaching and education. It felt as though life was finally aligning the stars for me. With the support of my family and a renewed sense of purpose, I enrolled in a local college, taking classes that deepened my understanding of educational theory, child development, and cultural diversity in the classroom. Juggling my studies, work at P.S. 182, and the responsibilities of motherhood was no small feat, but I embraced the challenge wholeheartedly. Each day was filled with a mix of lectures, lesson planning, and cherishing moments with my children.

My commitment to education fueled my passion, and I found ways to apply what I learned in class directly to my role at the school. I designed engaging activities that not only fostered a love of learning but also celebrated the unique backgrounds of my students. My experiences as a mother and educator allowed me to connect with my students on a deeper level, treating them with compassion and understanding.

As I progressed through my coursework, I was met with challenges—late nights spent studying, balancing family commitments, and navigating the occasional self-doubt. Yet, I drew strength from the support of my colleagues at P.S. 182 and my growing confidence. My fellow teachers admired my dedication and often turned to me for insights on creating a culturally responsive classroom environment. With each passing semester, my resolve only solidified. I was determined not only to obtain my certification but also to break down barriers for children who faced societal challenges. Inspired by my own journey and those of my students, I envisioned a future where every child, regardless of their background, had access to quality education and opportunities to succeed.

The realization of my dream was further reinforced by my interactions with Eric's father, who encouraged my academic pursuits. He recognized the tireless effort and determination I poured into my work and education, often reminding me of my brilliance and potential. Our supportive partnership blossomed as we shared responsibilities and navigated the challenges of parenting together.

As my college years progressed, I formed invaluable relationships with classmates who shared my passion for education. We engaged in discussions that inspired bold ideas about inclusive teaching and community engagement. These collaborative experiences sparked initiatives aimed at bridging gaps between diverse communities, reinforcing my belief in the power of education as a vehicle for change.

Eventually, the day came when I completed my studies—a culmination of hard work, perseverance, and dreams fulfilled. Family and friends gathered to celebrate my achievement, and the day felt monumental. My children, bustling with excitement, beamed with pride. My achievement symbolized all my sacrifices and dedication.

I became even more involved in my community and school. My newfound credentials opened doors for career advancement within the Board of Education, allowing me to take on more influential roles. I continued to inspire my children and students, emphasizing the value of education and serving as a guiding light for those striving to achieve their dreams.

With every step I took, I understood that my journey was part of a greater narrative—one where love, resilience, and the commitment to education could forge a better future. As I transitioned from being a teacher's assistant to a full-fledged educator, I remained deeply committed to shaping young minds and fostering a sense of hope in every child I taught.

Brooklyn became a canvas for my dreams, where I found purpose, joy, and a profound connection to my community. The challenges I faced along the way only served to solidify my mission—to advocate for all children, ensuring they had the nurturing, inclusive, and empowering education they deserved. I had turned my vision into reality, a journey marked by determination and the unwavering belief that with love and knowledge, anything was possible.

As I settled into my new role as an educator in Brooklyn, I became acutely aware of the evolving landscape of education in New York City. In 1969, a significant milestone occurred with the establishment of the United Federation of Teachers (UFT) for paraprofessionals, a development that resonated deeply with me and my colleagues at P.S. 182.

The formation of the UFT offered a vital space for paraprofessionals to voice their concerns, advocate for their rights, and seek better working conditions. As an educator who had risen through the ranks from a teacher's assistant to a fully certified paraprofessional, I felt a strong sense of solidarity with my fellow paraprofessionals. The establishment of the union was not just a professional advancement for me; it symbolized a broader movement toward recognizing the essential role that support staff played in the classroom.

I joined my colleagues in the initial meetings organized by the UFT, eager to learn more about our rights and the benefits the union could provide. I listened intently as experienced educators spoke passionately about the necessity of fair wages, access to training, and job security. The discussions illuminated the challenges often faced by paraprofessionals, who were essential in building supportive learning environments yet often lacked recognition and support.

Motivated by a desire to see my colleagues thrive, I became an active participant in union efforts. I engaged in planning sessions, helped organize workshops, and collaborated with fellow union members to ensure that our voices would be heard. Through my dedication, I reinforced the idea that every educator—regardless of title—was integral to the educational journey of children.

As I contributed to the union's initiatives, I experienced the powerful impact of collective action. Our advocacy resulted in meaningful changes: increased access to professional development training, more equitable pay, and enhanced support for our vital work in the classroom. This newfound sense of empowerment invigorated me and my peers, uniting us in a common cause—a shared mission that transcended individual roles in education.

During this period, I also found opportunities to mentor new paraprofessionals entering the field. With many fresh faces joining the UFT, I embraced my role as a guide and advocate, leveraging my own experiences to help others navigate the complexities of their roles in education. I offered insights on fostering positive relationships with teachers, developing inclusive classroom practices, and creating effective communication strategies with families.

Outside of my work, I stayed firmly grounded in my own children's lives. With Eric growing up alongside his siblings, I ensured that they were aware of the changes happening in the education landscape. I encouraged them to understand the importance of advocating for themselves and others, instilling values of equity and justice that I had come to embrace throughout my journey.

The union's emphasis on advocacy resonated with me personally as I continued to teach. I incorporated lessons on social justice, equality, and community participation into my curriculum. By doing so, I aimed to inspire my students to recognize their own voices and the power they held to effect change. The UFT's mission of supporting the rights of educators went hand-in-hand with my passion for nurturing the minds of the next generation.

My involvement with the UFT and my ongoing dedication to mentoring and advocacy became a cornerstone of my professional life. Through these efforts, I sought to create an environment where both educators and students could thrive, united by the shared values of equity, justice, and the transformative power of education.

As the momentum of the union grew, so did my resolve to contribute to a brighter future for education. I participated in rallies and pushed for policies that addressed the needs of marginalized communities. My commitment not only strengthened my footing within the UFT but also amplified my impact as an educator, reinforcing my dedication to nurturing an inclusive learning environment.

In this landscape of change, I found myself thriving. The establishment of the UFT served as a catalyst for my growth both professionally and personally. With every step forward, I continued to champion the rights of educators, placing a strong emphasis on the significance of community, relationships, and advocacy.

Brooklyn had transformed into a place of empowerment not just for me, but for countless others striving for recognition and support within the educational system. United by a shared mission, the voices of educators—especially paraprofessionals—began to echo louder, creating waves of change within our schools and beyond. I embraced my role within this movement, confident that together, we could forge a brighter, more equitable future for all who walked through the doors of the classroom.

As I continued my journey at P.S. 182, I felt a deep sense of responsibility to ensure that my students understood the richness and significance of their cultural heritage. With the establishment of Black History Month gaining momentum across the nation, I recognized an invaluable opportunity to create educational programming that celebrated the contributions, stories, and triumphs of African Americans. Motivated by my own experiences and the stories of resilience woven into my family's history, I set out to implement a comprehensive Black History curriculum at P.S. 182. I envisioned a month filled with engaging activities that would not only educate my students but also foster a sense of pride in their own identities.

I began by assembling a committee with fellow teachers, administrators, and interested parents, eager to collaboratively shape a meaningful program. I advocated for dedicated time and resources to spotlight the stories and impacts of notable figures in Black history, emphasizing the importance of representation in the classroom.

Throughout meetings, my passion shone through as I shared ideas about inviting local historians and community leaders to speak with students, hosting art exhibits that depicted important moments in Black history, and organizing performances that celebrated African American culture. The vision was met with enthusiasm, and the team worked diligently to bring it to life.

In the lead-up to February, I coordinated a series of lessons that highlighted influential figures such as Harriet Tubman, Frederick Douglass, Martin Luther King Jr., Rosa Parks, and many others. Each classroom at P.S. 182 was encouraged to explore one historical figure in depth, transforming the school into a vibrant tapestry of stories, art, and music.

In my own classroom, I crafted a curriculum that engaged my students in creative projects. They produced presentations, art displays, and even performances that showcased not only historical facts but also the cultural significance behind each figure's contributions. I made sure to connect these histories to the lives of my students, drawing parallels that made the learning relevant and personal. "Understanding where we come from helps us navigate where we're going," I often explained, encouraging my students to explore their own backgrounds and share their family stories. I created an inclusive atmosphere where every child felt valued, allowing them to express pride in their heritage and identity.

As February approached, the energy and excitement throughout the school grew. Our committee worked hard to finalize details for a school-wide celebration that would serve as the culmination of our efforts. It would include a multicultural fair, where families could set up booths representing their unique cultures, share traditional foods, and showcase cultural artifacts.

On the day of the celebration, the hallways of P.S. 182 were transformed. Banners covered the walls, adorned with art reflecting the historical figures studied. Students donned festive clothing inspired by their cultural backgrounds, and the air was filled with the sounds of music, laughter, and stories being shared.

I watched with immense pride as my students took center stage to present what they had learned. They passionately recited speeches, performed skits, and showcased the artwork they had created, encapsulating the spirit of Black History Month. Families filled the auditorium, their faces beaming with pride as they saw their children shine.

As the event unfolded, I felt a profound sense of fulfillment wash over me. The initiative I had championed not only enriched my students' understanding of their own identities but also fostered a deeper appreciation for the diversity that surrounded them. The stories of our ancestors resonated through the hallways, creating a legacy of pride and empowerment for future generations.

Beyond the celebration, the impact of these efforts echoed throughout the school year. My commitment to Black history instilled a cultural awareness that transcended February, encouraging students and faculty to continue exploring issues of equality, justice, and representation. I became a beloved figure in the school, not only for my dedication to education but also for the profound changes I championed. I created a foundation that helped foster open dialogue surrounding history, cultural heritage, and the significance of understanding one's roots.

In the years that followed, the legacy of Black History Month at P.S. 182 continued to flourish, becoming an annual tradition that celebrated the contributions of Black individuals to American society. My efforts inspired other schools in the district to implement similar programs, furthering the ripple effects of my passion for education and advocacy. Brooklyn was not just a backdrop to my journey; it became a canvas for change, a community where my vision transformed lives and inspired generations. My dedication to fostering understanding, representation, and pride in cultural heritage flooded the hallways of P.S. 182 with light, hope, and a commitment to build bridges across communities.

Years later, as I reflected on my journey from Mississippi to Brooklyn, I understood that the paths I navigated were not just about my own growth; they were about lifting others and ensuring that every child felt valued, proud, and empowered to make their mark on the world. Through education, advocacy, and cultural celebration, I carved a legacy—one that would continue to inspire future generations to celebrate their identities and the rich history that shaped us all.

After the success of my initiatives at P.S. 182, my journey as an educator led me to a new opportunity at P.S. 158. The transition was filled with fresh excitement and the potential for even greater impact, and I was eager to build upon the foundation I had established in my previous role. With my new position, I was determined to continue celebrating Black history and amplifying the voices of my students and their contributions to society.

Drawing on my past experiences, I quickly set about organizing a more expansive Black History Month program for P.S. 158. I envisioned a celebration that not only highlighted influential figures but also engaged the school community in meaningful discussions about relevance, activism, and social justice—topics that aligned with my commitment to advocacy.

Understanding the profound influence of guest speakers in motivating students, I focused on inviting prominent figures who could inspire both the students and the staff. That's when I reached out to the renowned civil rights leader, Jesse Jackson, hoping to provide the students with firsthand insights from someone who had dedicated his life to fighting for equality and justice.

As word spread about the possibility of Jesse Jackson's visit, anticipation grew among the students and staff alike. I believed that his message of hope, resilience, and activism would resonate deeply within our school. To build excitement, I collaborated with the school administration to promote the event, incorporating discussions and preparatory lessons that would help students engage with his ideas meaningfully.

On the day of Jesse Jackson's visit, the atmosphere at P.S. 158 was electric. Students gathered in the auditorium, buzzing with excitement and curiosity. I dedicated myself to ensuring everything was organized—from seating arrangements to technical requirements, making sure that every detail was taken care of ahead of time.

When Jesse Jackson arrived, the energy in the room shifted. His presence commanded attention, and his charisma immediately drew the students in. I introduced him, sharing a brief overview of his outstanding contributions to the civil rights movement and emphasizing the importance of his work in inspiring future generations.

Jackson spoke passionately, weaving together personal narratives and broader messages of hope and resilience. He encouraged my students to believe in themselves and to use their voices in advocating for change. "You are the leaders of tomorrow," he declared, urging them to take action in their communities and stand up against injustice.

As he shared stories of his experiences, the room grew quieter, and I could see the students engrossed in his words. I observed the rapt attention on their faces and felt proud of the platform we had created to foster such meaningful dialogue.

After his inspiring speech, Jackson opened the floor for questions, igniting a lively discussion. Students asked about his experiences, his motivations, and his advice for young activists. I guided the conversation, ensuring that every voice was heard. The interactions left a lasting impression on my students, many of whom felt inspired to take further steps in their own activist journeys. I saw a spark of determination in their eyes, and I knew the seeds of change had been planted.

Following the event, I organized reflection sessions where students could discuss what they had learned from Jackson and how they could apply those lessons to their own lives. Some expressed a desire to work on community service projects, while others wanted to start student-led initiatives focused on social justice issues. As the celebration of Black History Month progressed, I incorporated my students' ideas, turning the inspiration derived from Jackson's visit into actionable plans. We set up committees to work on various projects within the school and the community, fostering a sense of ownership and empowerment among the students. P.S. 158 became a hub for enthusiasm and engagement, reminding me that the influence of education extended far beyond textbooks. Together, we created a space where dialogue, culture, and advocacy united to foster hope for the future.

Looking back on my journey from Mississippi to Brooklyn and now at P.S. 158, I felt a deep sense of fulfillment. I have had the privilege of educating my students and instilling in them the belief that they can effect change in their communities. In every initiative, from celebrating Black history to inviting figures like Jesse Jackson, I reaffirmed my commitment to advocacy, education, and the empowerment of young minds.

With each passing year, my initiatives left indelible marks on my students, shaping their understanding of history and their roles as active participants in society. I stood as a beacon of hope for them, guiding them toward a future where they could embrace their identities, challenge injustices, and inspire others along the way. It was a legacy of education, empowerment, and advocacy that would resonate not only within the walls of P.S. 158 but throughout the broader community, ensuring that the stories of their ancestors lived on in their hearts and actions.

By 1977, I found myself in my early forties, reflecting on a life filled with resilience, challenges, and profound lessons learned along the way. My journey has been steeped in hardship and heartbreak, yet I emerged stronger and more determined than ever to make a difference in the lives of others.

My early years were marked by loss. The death of my father when I was just six years old left a void that shaped my childhood. Forced to navigate the world without his guidance, I found myself leaning into the strength that my mother exemplified, even as our lives were complicated by her struggles with mental illness. This created a sense of instability in my formative years, often leaving me feeling isolated and uncertain.

As I grew up, I battled the shadows of grief and loneliness, grappling with the realities of my surroundings. The racial discrimination I faced in my hometown weighed heavily on my spirit, amplifying my feelings of despair. Those experiences left deep scars, influencing my understanding of the inequalities that permeated society. The longing for a sense of belonging and acceptance fueled my resolve to seek change in both my life and the lives of those around me.

The separation from my husband added another layer of complexity to my emotional landscape. While our paths had diverged, I knew that our decision stemmed from the hardships we faced. The weight of societal pressures, combined with personal struggles, had created a rift that often felt insurmountable. I found solace in my children, pouring my heart into their upbringing and ensuring they felt loved and secure amidst the chaos.

With each passing year, my experiences deepened my understanding of life's challenges. From the loss of my father to my mother's struggles, the intersection of grief and hope shaped my perspective. I began to recognize how these struggles could be sources of strength rather than solely sources of despair.

In the process of healing, I sought ways to channel my pain into something powerful. Teaching at P.S. 158 became not just my profession but my purpose. My interactions with students were founded on empathy and compassion, rooted in my own life's journey. As I shared lessons drawn from my experiences, I encouraged my students to recognize their own challenges and to embrace their identities with confidence.

In an unexpected turn of events, my healing journey led me to understand that sharing my story was not just a way to cope—it was a means to empower others. I began to speak at community gatherings and events, discussing my life, the hardships I had overcome, and the importance of resilience in the face of adversity, believing that sharing my truth could inspire others to confront their struggles head-on.

My speeches resonated with many. realized that my story reflected the narratives of countless others—those who had faced loss, discrimination, and emotional turmoil. I spoke passionately about the importance of mental health, advocating for understanding and compassion toward those who were suffering. Through my vulnerability, I aimed to dismantle the stigma surrounding mental illness and encouraged others to seek help.

My journey of self-discovery intertwined with my mission to foster an inclusive community. incorporated discussions about mental health and racial discrimination into my work at P.S. 158, fostering open dialogue among students and staff. The understanding cultivated through my own experiences helped create a safe environment where students could share their feelings and learn from one another.

As I reflected on my life's hardships, I grew to understand the profound teachings that lay beneath the surface of pain. The love of my children, my work as an educator, and the connections I forged in my community became my pillars of strength. I believed that despite the struggles, there was always a pathway to healing—one that included love, hope, and the willingness to advocate for change.

By 1977, I had paved a path toward empowerment, using my voice to inspire growth and understanding. The hardships I had experienced became not just stories of adversity but testaments to resilience, advocacy, and transformation. I embraced my role as a storyteller, an educator, and a champion for the voiceless.

Looking forward, I felt called to delve deeper into my advocacy work. I envisioned a future where my experiences could lead to meaningful change—where mental health resources were accessible and where discussions on racial equality were the norm, not the exception. My determination fueled my dream of creating spaces for healing and understanding so that others might not have to endure what I had faced alone.

In sharing my journey, I became a beacon of hope for those navigating their own hardships. The story of my life is not just about overcoming obstacles; it's about thriving amidst adversity, using my past to forge a brighter future, and empowering others along the way. Each step I take is a testament to my unwavering spirit and commitment to advocacy—an illumination of a heart dedicated to making the world a better place for generations to come.

Moving to Far Rockaway marked a significant chapter in my life, one framed by tranquility and a sense of community. Nestled near the beach, I found a restful haven where the gentle sound of the waves served as a reminder of nature's healing power. Here, in this vibrant seaside community, I continued my work with the Board of Education at Far Rockaway High School, intertwining my passion for education with my commitment to serving others.

As I settled into my role at the high school, I felt invigorated by the opportunities to foster meaningful change within the student body and the local community. Drawing on my extensive experiences, I identified gaps in resources and support for students, particularly in the areas of mental health, academic enrichment, and cultural awareness. Motivated by my past, I was determined to create programs that would empower students and help them navigate their educational journeys. My goal was to educate students and raise awareness about mental health by helping organize events where mental health professionals could speak to both students and parents.

Another initiative I launched was a mentorship program, pairing students with community leaders and higher education mentors who could provide guidance and support. This program facilitated the sharing of experiences and knowledge, enabling students to envision a brighter future for themselves. I believe in the power of representation, and by connecting students with mentors from similar backgrounds, I sought to enhance their confidence and ambition.

My dedication did not go unnoticed. The impact of my initiatives resonated throughout Far Rockaway High School, earning me numerous accolades from both students and faculty members. Several principals recognized my commitment to improving the educational experience, awarding me recognition for my instrumental role in fostering a positive school environment.

My efforts also extended beyond the school, reaching the wider Far Rockaway community. Local councilman Donovan Richards paid tribute to my impactful work, presenting me with a Proclamation in acknowledgment of my initiatives and dedication to service. I couldn't have been more proud to receive an honor from someone I had watched rise through the ranks to become the borough president of Queens, reflecting both my commitment to service and the spirit of community upliftment.

With each award and accolade, I felt a profound sense of gratitude. These recognitions were not simply reminders of my hard work; they were testaments to the transformative power of community and education. I understood that every achievement was a stepping stone, paving the way for a better future for my family and the students I served.

As my reputation as an educator and community advocate grew, I envisioned expanding my reach even further. I collaborated with local organizations, fostering partnerships that connected students with resources for internships, scholarships, and summer programs. Through these partnerships, I aimed to bridge the gap between education and employment, providing students with real-world experiences that would enhance their skills and prepare them for future success.

Beyond my professional endeavors, I took immense pride in my family. Each accomplishment I achieved was not only for myself but also for my children, who served as my inspiration. I instilled in them the values of hard work, perseverance, and service, ensuring they understood the importance of giving back to their community.

At home, I often engaged my children in discussions about my advocacy work, sharing stories of the students whose lives had been touched by our initiatives. This not only kept my children connected to my work but also inspired them to seek ways to contribute meaningfully to their own community. In Far Rockaway, my life has been characterized by a strong sense of purpose, dedication, and love. I foster a sense of belonging for my students, my community, and my family.

Every day, I walk the hallways of Far Rockaway High School with pride, knowing that my work will help build a more promising future for generations to come. My unwavering commitment to serving my community with dignity and gratitude continues to shine brightly, a testament to a life enhanced by purpose, resilience, and the transformative power of education.

I understand that the waves that lap against the shore signify not only the tranquility of my surroundings but also the relentless drive for change that I carry within me. Each tide brings new challenges and new opportunities, and I am ready to embrace them all. Through my work, my story has become a beacon of hope, inspiring others to believe in the potential for change and the incredible impact one dedicated individual can have on a community.

At 90 years old, I found myself reflecting deeply on the remarkable journey of my life. I felt an overwhelming desire to share my story and the lessons I had learned. With each passing day, I dedicated myself to telling my story—a heartfelt memoir that would illuminate my experiences and offer hope to others facing their own adversities.

I envisioned this book as a beacon of encouragement for those grappling with life's challenges. I aimed to convey the powerful message that no matter the circumstances—whether it be loss, discrimination, or personal struggles—one can overcome adversity through resilience, faith, and the support of the community. I wanted my words to resonate with readers, instilling in them the belief that they, too, could forge their own paths toward healing and empowerment.

I have always been a God-fearing woman, and my faith has served as the foundation upon which I built my life. In all my endeavors, I attribute my strength to my relationship with God, drawing from that well of faith to guide me through the most difficult times. My life's work had transcended mere accomplishments. It had become a message of love, empowerment, and the enduring spirit of a woman who knew that no matter the storms I weathered, I would always rise to meet the dawn. And so, my celebration resonated beyond the day, inspiring everyone present to walk their paths with courage and conviction—just as I have done throughout my extraordinary life. I took a deep breath, gathering the words that had been in my heart for so long. "Thank you to each and every one of you who have touched my life. Your love, support, and presence have shaped who I am today."

I looked around at the familiar faces, recalling the memories and lessons shared over the years. I felt immense gratitude for my family, who have stood by me through every storm and celebrated every triumph. They have been the strength that buoyed me during difficult moments, the laughter that lightened my days, and the love that filled my heart.

Turning to my friends, I expressed my appreciation for their unwavering support and companionship. "You have been my anchors, my confidants, and my cheerleaders, "Thank you for believing in me, even when I doubted myself."

Next, I acknowledged my co-workers and colleagues—those who walked with me in the education field, striving to uplift young minds. "Together, we have made a difference, and our collective efforts have truly created a lasting impact in our community.

Finally, I turned my gratitude to the prayer warriors—those who have prayed for me, with me, and over me throughout my life. "Your faith and prayers have been my lifeline, "In times of darkness, you brought light, and in moments of doubt, you restored hope. Thank you for your unwavering trust in God and for the strength you have given me through your prayers."

Dear heavenly Father, I come before you with a heart full of gratitude for the gift of life and love. Thank you for allowing us to gather here today to celebrate the gift of 90 incredible years. I am grateful for the connections I share, the challenges I have overcome, and the countless blessings you have bestowed upon me.

Lord, thank you for my family, my friends, and all those who have walked with me through this journey. I pray for each person here—may they be filled with your love, grace, and peace. Help us to carry forward the spirit of kindness and compassion, empowering us to make a positive impact in the lives of others just as we have the privilege of impacting one another.

As I move forward from this day, I ask that you continue to guide me, giving me the strength to face life's challenges with faith and resilience. Help me to be a light in this world, to share my story, and to lift others up. May I always remember that with you by my side, I can overcome any adversity.

In your holy name, I pray.Amen

In closing, I realized that my legacy would live on—through the stories I have shared, the lives I have touched, and the unbreakable bonds formed with everyone gathered. As I prepared to embark on this new chapter, I held the cherished memories of my past and looked forward to the future with hope, love, and an unwavering spirit of gratitude. Thank you to all who have shared in my story and contributed to the incredible tapestry of my life.

To my seven children: Curtis, Joe, Michael, Hyrtecene II, Jeanette, Nathaniel, and Eric. Each of you brings me joy, your dreams ignited my hopes, and their struggles stirred my unwavering support.

Curtis, with his adventurous spirit, filled my days with excitement, while Joe, ever the compassionate one, teaches me the true meaning of empathy. Michael's creativity illuminated our home, inspiring me to embrace imagination. Hyrtecene II, a reflection of my own strength, carries forward my legacy with pride. Jeanette's determination pushed me to be resilient, and Nathaniel's curiosity reminds me of life's endless possibilites. Eric, the youngest, represented my dreams yet to unfold, bringing a sense of wonder into my life.

Pictures of my husband and our children.

Family gathering, Joe, Curtis, me, Eric, Danny, Lil Herty and Mike and the picture on the wall is a drawing of my grandson, Richie who is no longer with us, He will be remember for a lifetime, his motto is Live, Laugh and Love ♥♥♥

A heartfelt thank you to my daughter, Lil Herty for writing my memoir. Your dedication, love, and effort in capturing my story mean the world to me. You have not only preserved my memories but also brought them to life in a way that I could never have done alone. I'm grateful for your support and creativity, and I cherish the bond we share through this incredible journey. Thank you for being my storyteller.

PHOTOS

Martha & George

The story of Martha & George is one that throughout the years in the 1800's their love story became a poignant reminder of resilience in the face of adversity- a testament to how love can flourish even in the darkest of times. My family tree is the Smith's, Jones and Fishers.

Aunt Annie, a true pillar of strength and love in our family, lived a remarkable 107 years. Her life was a testament to faith, kindness, and selflessness, leaving an indelible mark on all who were fortunate enough to know her. As we carry her legacy forward, may we always remember the profound impact she had on our lives and strive to embody her spirit of love, devotion, and generosity. Aunt Annie's memory will forever be a source of inspiration and joy, guiding us with her shining example of a life well-lived.

Aunt Mattie's presence in my family's heritage was a true gift, adorning it with grace, dignity, respect, and an abundance of love. Her unmatched qualities have enriched our lives in ways that words can barely capture.

My family, on the right is me, my cousin Jr. sitting on the floor and my two nieces, Matilda and Mary, Lil Herty, My mom holding my son Eric, next to him is Stanley, my sister and her twin daughters Deloris and Doris and my son Curtis.

My sons, Curtis, Mike, Joe and Eric in the early 70's

The Early years of me working for the Board of Education

A POEM OF MY JOURNEY

The Beginning

In the heart of the Southern land,
Where cotton blooms and rivers wend,
My roots run deep, my story weaves,
A tapestry of strength that never leaves.
Born under the Crescent Moon's soft glow,
In a land where magnolias grow,
I am the echo of ancestors past,
Their struggles and triumphs forever last.
From chains and lashes, we arose,
Through trials and tears, our spirit glows,
Resilient souls, unbowed and free,
African American, proud as can be.
In the hymns of gospel sung with grace,
In the rhythm of drums, I find my place,
In the sweet taste of cornbread and greens,
In the whispers of history, yet unseen.
I am the promise of a rising sun,
A legacy of battles fought and won,
In each heartbeat, a rhythm true,
My beginnings speak of strength anew.
So let my voice soar, let my story be told,
Of struggle, of triumph, of spirit bold,
African American, proud and strong,
In the South where my roots have grown,
I claim my heritage, soul fully known,
From cotton fields to freedom's throne,
A land of promise, where I was born.

"I can't thank you enough for being there when I needed it most."

www.ingramcontent.com/pod-product-compliance
Lightning Source LLC
Chambersburg PA
CBHW040848120626
46547CB00001B/78